New cinema in Britain

Designed by Gillian Greenwood

Roger Manvell

New cinema in Britain

studio vista | dutton pictureback
general editor David Herbert

Author's note

When I was asked to write this short history of the post-war British feature film, it was agreed that the major amount of space should be given to the more 'advanced' or 'experimental' films of the past ten years or so. This may perhaps explain why certain films are discussed more fully than others which are more famous, and with which in any case the reader is probably more familiar. Since this book is written for American as well as British readers, I have had on occasion to elaborate certain details which may seem over-obvious to people resident in Britain.

Since there is virtually no comprehensive history of the British feature film up to the present time, the range of the films included in this survey is relatively wide —though I could not, of course, include every film which has merit from one point of view or another. There are, after all, good reference books in which British directors and their films appear, for example those edited by Leslie Halliwell and Peter Graham, to say nothing of the monthly Bulletin of the British Film Institute. But I apologise to those who may find certain pages carrying a fair load of titles, and to those who may feel films they happen to like are omitted. I have also felt it necessary wherever possible to include reference to plots or situations, since younger readers, or those abroad, may well have missed seeing films with which older, home-based readers are familiar. There is always, too, the problem of deciding at what point to stop in a survey of this kind; in general, it may be taken to be the summer of 1968, though a few references or stills may over-step this.

I would like to express my gratitude to the British Council, to the editor of the *Humanist*, and to the Society of Film and Television Arts for permission to quote, in most cases, passages from writing I have undertaken for them. I would also like to acknowledge the very generous cooperation of the following in supplying stills: Academy Cinemas, Allied Artists, Anglo-Amalgamated, Associated British-Pathe, British Lion, Bryanston, BBC, Columbia, Compton-Cameo, Garrick, Independent, Institute of Contemporary Arts, Lion International, London Independent Producers, Metro-Goldwyn-Mayer, National Film Archive, Paramount, Planet, RKO-Radio, Rank Organisation, Republic, 20th-Century-Fox United Artists, Universal-International and Warner-Pathe.

R.M.

Frontispiece

The Touchables 1968. Director Bob Freeman

Published in London by Studio Vista Limited
Blue Star House, Highgate Hill, N19
and in New York by E. P. Dutton and Co Inc
201 Park Avenue South, New York 3, NY
Distributed in Canada by General Publishing Co Ltd
30 Lesmill Road, Don Mills, Ontario
Set in 8D on 9 pt Univers, 2 pts leaded
Made and printed in Great Britain by
Richard Clay (The Chaucer Press), Ltd, Bungay, Suffolk

SBN 289 79607 5 (paperback)
SBN 289 79608 3 (hardback)

Contents

Lord of the Flies 1961–3. Director Peter Brook

Points of view

The British film industry has always seemed to operate inside a hornet's nest. This is because so many of the people involved—creative people, non-creative people, businessmen, trade unionists, politicians, distributors, exhibitors, publicists, critics, highly vocal fans, to say nothing of economists and members of official committees of enquiry—often hold totally divergent views about what it is and what it should be. Most of what they say is near enough correct, given their disparate points of view. But this does not help. It merely contributes to the eternal 'problem' which 'the industry' represents.

It should hardly be necessary to point out that, as part of a capitalist economy, the film industry must make money in order to exist. In this it does not differ from other industries which depend on producing goods for the consumer market. The film industry's perennial problems begin with the fact that each feature film produced* is a prototype and has to blaze its own trail with the public. As everyone knows through endless repetition, films are increasingly costly to make, and yet a very modest proportion of the box-office takings (about one-fifth) filters back to the producer, the man who has, after all, taken the initial risk in promoting the film. Setting up an 'independent' film venture—and most of the interesting British films have for long been the work of the so-called independents, producers operating outside the authority of a large production company—has been compared to the financial process involved in setting up a merchant-venturer's ship in the seventeenth century. The money is brought together piece-meal, loans here and investments there, and you gamble on the good ship enjoying a fair passage through the relatively uncharted seas and bringing back profitable goods intact. And there was a time when a little piracy on the side didn't go amiss.

It was the dishonest, mushroom producers of the 1930s which led to the establishment of a tough trade union, while the eternal slumps and booms with their uneven production record during the post-war decade gave most film technicians in the feature industry, however skilled, one of the least secure, if highest paid,

* The annual average production of first feature films in Britain during the past ten years has stood at around 75.

forms of employment in Britain. To complicate matters, the British film industry (though reckoned, rightly, a cultural asset nationally) has never ceased to look like a sick man who is passed on from one puzzled specialist to another. Successive governments of the right and the left have probed and prodded it, and successive governments have even gone so far as to administer some injections—the National Film Finance Corporation established in 1948, the British Film Production Fund set up in 1950, and the abolition of cinema entertainments duty in 1960.

In comparison with some other major film-producing countries, the pattern of British film-making may well appear conservative. There is nothing like the room for manoeuvre that there is, for example, in France. Whereas France has an open internal market for production and distribution, Britain is firmly segmented by the all-powerful exhibition circuits which have strong links with distribution as well as production itself. It is well known that no independent producer can hope to see his money back on a normally (if modestly) budgeted feature film unless it is accepted by one or other of the two prime circuits—that of the Rank Organisation or that of Associated British Cinemas, representing between them approaching 600 of the best theatres in Britain's total of some 1,700. This means that if a film like Peter Brook's *Lord of the Flies,* Clive Donner's *The Caretaker,* or Desmond Davis's *The Uncle* appears to the circuit selectors to lack wider audience appeal and is therefore rejected, it may be left unshown on the shelf until eventually it slips before the public via one or other of the specialised cinemas. Here, however popular it may prove to be with the intelligentsia, it can earn for its producer only a minute fraction of its costs.

The main fault of the British exhibition pattern has been lack of resilience, its almost total inability to cope adequately with any kind of film the appeal of which lies at some point between the main stream of broad, popular taste and the taste of the minority who patronise the specialised (or art house) cinemas—that is, between the public enumerated in millions and that counted in tens of thousands. This is a situation unique to the film as an art, and to some extent unique to the film in Britain, at least as far as the leading film-producing countries of Western Europe are concerned.

Everywhere, the pressures on the film-maker are considerable—to conform commercially, to conform to the censorship, to conform politically, to conform socially and not offend pressure-groups with particular influence. Above all, perhaps, the pressure on him is to be consistently successful, never to make a film which will send him back to square one in his career, or ditch him altogether. True, similar pressures weigh on the dramatist and the book-writer—but because the costs of production for books and even for plays are so much less, the naked impact of the pressures to be successful slacken. The theatre, too, is the darling of the more advanced communities, even in Britain, which has been notoriously mean to the arts at the official level. Yet few in Britain quarrel with subsidy to opera, to the National Theatre, to the Royal Shakespeare Company, and so forth; it enables them to produce of their best above and beyond what they can earn in hard cash from public patronage at the box-office. But the film-maker, however meritorious as an artist, is left to stand on his own feet, virtually unaided. Governments in Britain have come to the conclusion that the film is too tricky a business to subsidise, and so must be left to solve its own problems, and most state intervention, such as it has been, has done little to assist those who stood most in need of it. By far the greater part of the film production fund in its present and previous forms has disappeared in subsidy to those who have in any case already done well at the box-office or, in present conditions, companies representing wealthy American production interests.

Admittedly, the British film industry has proved a singularly difficult one to help owing, as we have seen, to the divergent voices which represent it. Many extreme remedies have been at various times proposed—nationalise the whole thing, dissolve the larger cinema circuits, create a third, competitive circuit, introduce anti-Trust laws similar to those which gave a new structure to the industry in the United States, bring in various legal enforcements which oblige recalcitrant exhibitors to show films which, left to their own better judgment, they would never dream of showing. What people of good will are trying to devise is some system which would enable promising artistic projects to reach production stage and, once completed, to be shown in suitable circumstances throughout the country.

The story of British feature-film production, therefore, is also the story of the courage, pertinacity and imagination of a considerable number of men who have insisted on maintaining quality in their work, often in spite of every conceivable discouragement. If most of the achievement in all but the most recent British films has been on the conservative, or academic levels, the reason for this is, as I have shown, that the creative men and the financial interests on which they are dependent have managed to find in this kind of film their largest measure of common ground. This is characteristic of the best British film-making of the 1940s and 1950s. More recently, in the 1960s, other factors again have come into play which have widened, and shaken, the taste of those who provide finance for films. However, the tough, lively and 'vulgar' cultural revolution which has taken possession of Britain largely during the 1960s found its antecedents in the 1950s mainly outside the cinema. This change, or widening in public taste, was to enable the film-makers who wanted to do so to introduce new styles of production into the cinemas and still be successful at the box-office. The pattern was not to be nearly so revolutionary as the 'new wave' and its aftermath in France, but revolutionary it nevertheless was for so innately conservative a country as Britain.

This cultural revolution was to a considerable degree eased over by television, or rather by what television accustomed the British public to accept as entertainment from a screen. In spite of the continual emphasis on what is new and strange and unheard-of in the average publicist's jargon, nothing is more conservative than popular entertainment; this is true of most countries, even the United States, with its reputation for seizing with avidity on anything divertingly new. The public learns to respond to a certain range of subjects, forms and idioms, and tends to regard anything foreign to these as outlandish and, in consequence, *un*entertaining. Television has to endure only too many unhealthy pressures, but these do not include the harsh immediacies of the daily box-office. It could afford (indeed, it was forced) to experiment with new writers, directors, actors and idioms, and from the later 1950s was increasingly successful in both drama and drama-documentary in opening up new, mainly realistic forms of entertainment. British television drama and documentary are universally acknowledged to be among the most advanced in the world, and the cinema was to recruit new talent widely from this younger and more progressive medium during the 1960s.

The British film industry, which, like the American, gained so much talent from Continental Europe during the period of Hitler, also gained further talent from the United States during the period of McCarthy. A few writers and directors left the U.S. for good and settled in Britain, becoming makers of British films. Following the 'dispersion' of American film production during the 1950s, a consequence of the severance of production and exhibition following the anti-Trust laws, the decline in feature production, and the increasing dedication of Hollywood to making purely television films, both the independent producers and the recognised companies saw the advantage of producing films in the European studios, where the costs, especially at first, were significantly easier than in the United States.* In the case of Britain, the fulfilment of quota regulations in the use of British labour meant that American-sponsored films could rank, in Britain, as British and enjoy the status of British quota in the cinemas and draw on the subsidy of the Film Production Fund. As soon as these films left Britain, however, they would lose their specifically British status and become the same in foreign eyes as any other American picture. In 1967–8, for example, British production, both legally and technically, included Stanley Kubrick's space film *2001,* Fred Zinnemann's production of Robert Bolt's play, *A Man for all Seasons,* Henry Hathaway's *The Last Safari* (shot on location in Kenya), and Sidney Lumet's *The Deadly Affair.* How many of these, seen abroad, were promoted as British? American money has backed many very British-style films from *Lawrence of Arabia, Becket* and *The Pumpkin Eater* to *Tom Jones, The Knack* and the Beatles' films.

By 1969 it was estimated that up to 90 per cent of British films would in fact be American-sponsored, that is, have a greater or lesser degree of American money in their production. Although these dollar investments were very welcome to the hard-pressed British economy, the control of ostensibly British films from Hollywood (or Wall Street) is not so welcome to those who care for the cinema as an 'asset to British culture'. It also means that in the foreign markets the specific hallmark of British film-making is almost entirely disappearing. However, it must be recognised that in Europe as a whole co-production has become normal practice. What we are all concerned with is that, under the new forms of financial sponsorship, as many films as possible retain the valuable indigenous qualities which the various traditional cultures of

* See *A Competitive Cinema,* Terence Kelly (Institute of Economic Affairs 1966), Chapter V. Also, *New Cinema in the USA,* Roger Manvell (Studio Vista/Dutton, 1968), p. 27.

Europe possess. In any case, Britain has herself signed co-production agreements with France in 1965 and with Italy in 1967.

But what is meant by a 'national' cinema? A film, or for that matter any narrative or dramatic work, can become indigenous to a particular national culture on different planes or levels. It is not a matter of setting, but of style; Shakespeare's plays are set in any manner of locations, real or fictitious, but the style and thought belong to the England of his time. In much the same way *The Third Man*, set in Vienna but essentially created by two Englishmen, Graham Greene and Carol Reed, is very English in style and thought. On the other hand, *Dr Strangelove,* though legally British, is far from being indigenously so. If anything, this brilliant, 'dark' burlesque is as American as its prime creator, Stanley Kubrick. How indigenously Irish is Joseph Strick's film of *Ulysses*? We are proud to have had Joseph Losey working in this country for some years, but how indigenously British are *The Criminal, The Servant, King and Country* or *Accident,* or how much are they the particular vision of a particular man who has the observant, interpreting eye of an 'outsider'? While one is certain that, for example, *A Man for all Seasons* is very British indeed, what are *Fahrenheit 451, Cul-de-Sac, Blow-Up*? Subjects patently vary in the way they need to penetrate into the roots of their settings and reflect those qualities we regard as indigenous.

The international status of any industry can be graded both culturally and economically according to the degree of international penetration achieved by its films. This, of course, is what has made the American product of such outstanding importance in the history of the cinema—American films are shown virtually everywhere in the world, even in many of the communist countries, and they have been distributed in universal abundance ever since the period just before the first world war. However, since the 1950s Hollywood has no longer remained the monolithic centre for American production, and the number of American feature films produced annually has dropped to below half the former total. British feature films, though far less in number even than this diminished total, have during the past ten years steadily increased their reputation and popularity abroad and their favourable trading balance.

Behind the good academic or 'nationalistic' film, the spectacular production, or the ephemeral box-office 'attraction', lies an entirely new school of film-making which has yet to prove itself with the public. If America has her 'underground' movies which turn their back on everything 'normal' in the cinema and start from scratch with films as forms of wholly personal self-expression, so Britain is beginning (within professional film-making) to show signs of being able to sustain low-budget feature production of films which are much more personal in style and subject. They have a dual problem to meet—the oldest problem in the business, or the art, however you regard it. Can they find enough ready money to bring themselves to completion in production; can they, once produced, find profitable outlets and a wide enough public to sustain them? It is the point at which we came in.

A Man for All Seasons 1966. Director Fred Zinnemann
Orson Welles

Hamlet 1948 Director Laurence Olivier
Laurence Olivier

Post-war feature production

During the period following the war, the reputations of many directors who had become known before or during the war years were further established, including Carol Reed, David Lean, Thorold Dickinson, Michael Powell, Charles Frend, Frank Launder, Sidney Gilliat, John and Roy Boulting, and Anthony Asquith. Other prominent directors were Charles Crichton, Basil Dearden, Alexander Mackendrick, Leslie Norman, Jack Lee, Lewis Gilbert, Guy Hamilton, Roy Baker, Ralph Thomas, Ronald Neame, J. Lee Thompson and Henry Cornelius. Equally, certain stars emerged during the latter part of the war (or immediately post-war): notably, Eric Portman, John Mills, Rex Harrison, Richard Attenborough, Trevor Howard, Robert Newton, Stewart Granger, Alec Guinness, Michael Redgrave, James Mason, David Niven,

Robert Donat and Leo Genn. Laurence Olivier, of course, was to appear in all three of his Shakespearean productions, *Henry V*, *Hamlet* and *Richard III*. Other star players included Jack Hawkins, Richard Todd, Kenneth More, Dirk Bogarde, Richard Burton, Peter Finch, Anthony Quayle and Laurence Harvey. Among the actresses were Anna Neagle, Vivien Leigh, Ann Todd, Margaret Lockwood, Celia Johnson, Virginia McKenna, Margaret Leighton and Yvonne Mitchell.

Of the hundreds of films made in Britain during the years following the war it is impossible to list more than a few to represent the best. Such a list must include Carol Reed's *Odd Man*

Odd Man Out 1947. Director Carol Reed
F. J. McCormick

Out, The Fallen Idol and *The Third Man*; David Lean's two adaptations from Dickens, *Great Expectations* and *Oliver Twist*, and his other films, *The Sound Barrier* and *Hobson's Choice*; Noel Langley's adaptation of *The Pickwick Papers*, with James Hayter as an admirable Pickwick; Anthony Asquith's *The Browning Version* and *Carrington V.C.*; the famous Ealing comedies (a number of which established Alec Guinness as a major star), *Hue and Cry, Passport to Pimlico, Kind Hearts and Coronets, The Lavender Hill Mob, The Man in the White Suit, Whisky Galore* and

The Third Man 1949. Director Carol Reed
Joseph Cotten

Oliver Twist 1948. Director David Lean
Alec Guinness, Anthony Newley

Hue and Cry 1947. Director Charles Crichton

Pickwick Papers 1952. Director Noel Langley
James Hayter

Kind Hearts and Coronets 1949. Director Robert Hamer
Alec Guinness

The Lavender Hill Mob 1951. Director Charles Crichton
Alec Guinness

The Ladykillers, as well as one of the most successful macabre comedies to be made in Britain, *Dead of Night; Genevieve,* the comedy that brought Kenneth More to the forefront; the satirical farces of John and Roy Boulting and their serious thriller of the problems following a threat to London by a madman carrying a nuclear bomb, *Seven Days to Noon*; the 'location' films, Paul Rotha's Irish production, *No Resting Place, The Overlanders,* made by Harry Watt for Ealing in Australia, *Scott of the Antarctic,* directed by Charles Frend, with locations in Switzerland and

The Ladykillers 1955. Director Alexander Mackendrick
Alec Guinness, Katie Johnson, Peter Sellers, Danny Green

On pages 24/25
The Overlanders 1946. Director Harry Watt

Dead of Night 1945. Directors of episodes: Alberto Cavalcanti, Charles Crichton, Basil Dearden, Robert Hamer
Michael Redgrave

Seven Days to Noon 1950. Producer/Director John and Roy Boulting
Barry Jones

Genevieve 1953. Director Henry Cornelius
Kenneth More, Kay Kendall

Scott of the Antarctic 1948. Director Charles Frend

Cry, the Beloved Country 1951. Director Zoltan Korda
Lionel Ngakane, Canada Lee

Norway, and the African films, *Cry, the Beloved Country,* and *Simba* (Brian Desmond Hurst). War was portrayed in *The Cruel Sea, The Divided Heart, The Wooden Horse, The Colditz Story, The Dam Busters, The Small Back Room,* and *Odette.* Some early films about men in industry in the documentary style were *Chance of a Lifetime, The Blue Scar* and *The Brave Don't Cry.*

The Cruel Sea 1952. Director Charles Frend
Jack Hawkins

The Divided Heart 1954. Director Charles Crichton
Yvonne Mitchell

The Colditz Story 1955. Director Guy Hamilton

The Small Back Room 1948. Producer/Director Michael Powell and Emeric Pressburger
David Farrar

The Dam Busters 1955. Director Michael Anderson
Richard Todd, Michael Redgrave

Odette 1951. Director Herbert Wilcox
Anna Neagle

The Brave Don't Cry 1952. Director Philip Leacock
Fulton Mackay, Andrew Keir

The best 'period' films were probably Thorold Dickinson's *The Queen of Spades* (taken from Pushkin's short story) and Asquith's adaptation of Oscar Wilde's fantastic comedy, *The Importance of Being Earnest.* Peter Ustinov, while still in his twenties, wrote and directed *School for Secrets, Vice Versa* and *Private Angelo.* Striking (if sometimes artificial and mannered) films with great technical virtuosity came from Michael Powell and Emeric Pressburger, including *A Matter of Life and Death, Black Narcissus, The Red Shoes* and *Tales of Hoffman.* No list of representative post-war films would be complete without mention of

The Red Shoes 1948. Producer/Director Michael Powell and Emeric Pressburger
Leonide Massine

The Queen of Spades 1948. Director Thorold Dickinson
Anton Walbrook, Edith Evans

Animal Farm 1954. Producer/Director John Halas and Joy Batchelor

Animal Farm (John Halas and Joy Batchelor), the first feature-length animated film to be made in Britain, and unique as being a 'serious' cartoon adapted from George Orwell's celebrated fable.

A great deal, of course, depended on the screenwriters from whose original scripts and adaptations of novels and plays many of these films were produced. British films, however, have been very dependent on good scripts; original stories and screenplays remain rare, but include, for example, scripts by T. E. B. Clarke (among them, *Hue and Cry, Passport to Pimlico* and *The Lavender Hill Mob*), Graham Greene's story for *The Third Man,* and, much more recently, Frederic Raphael's script for *Darling* and Robert Bolt's for *Lawrence of Arabia.*

There was a period when British films became too script-bound, and the images on the screen were like a succession of paper kites tied to their script's apron-strings. The release came when directors and writers established a freer creative association with each other, and novelists and dramatists such as Harold Pinter, John Mortimer, David Mercer, Alan Sillitoe, David Storey, Edna O'Brien and Shelagh Delaney worked with their directors on the adaptation of their own or entirely original work for the screen. The younger generation of writers working primarily in the literary and dramatic world have a greater innate response than their predecessors to the very different needs of the cinema; they are more immediately responsive to a director's way of seeing the screen treatment of their work develop, and some may have had helpful experience in writing for television. But the hard fact remains that Britain's established directors have normally been men whose scripts did not originate from themselves but came either from professional screenwriters or from writers and dramatists who were invited to help adapt their already successful novels and plays into films. There could not, therefore, be a greater contrast between the films of, say, Antonioni, Fellini, Godard or Truffaut, and those of the established British film-makers. Though this may be partly the result of the temperament of our established directors, who are not *auteurs* in the French sense, it is also partly due to the method of financing films. Those who advance considerable sums of money against future production like to see a nicely typed and bound screenplay on their desks, together with an exciting star or two prepared to feature in it. And the stars themselves normally like to see a script before committing their reputations to a director's hands.

The later 1950s—the new phase

With the publication of the first novels of such writers as John Braine (*Room at the Top,* 1957), Alan Sillitoe (*Saturday Night and Sunday Morning,* 1958) and Stan Barstow (*A Kind of Loving,* 1960), and the first successful production of plays by John Osborne (*Look Back in Anger,* 1956) and Arnold Wesker (*Roots,* 1959), Britain was in for a cultural landslide. The adulation accorded these new writers and dramatists and the space given them in the 'quality' press, made it clear that their work stood for far more than its individual worth necessarily merited. Their initial value lay in their response to the unexpressed spirit of the period in which they lived and wrote; they had the good sense, or sensitivity, to assess the climate rightly and give it uncompromising, though sometimes uncontrolled, 'free-wheeling' expression. The cult of the 'angry young man' soon became tiresome largely because the press pushed it to the point of utter boredom, while the state of protest by the leading young men, who either were or posed as being angry, became ridiculous as they grew richer and richer through the public's lavish patronage of their protests. But their basic virtue still remained; they replaced (or supplemented, to put it more accurately) a worn-out, middle-class culture which had nothing fresh to say by a new and vigorous culture which derived its principal strength from the attitudes and values of the British working-class. The growing prosperity and purchasing power of the young working-class were making their voice and their tastes powerful in the land. Many of the new working-class writers and actors had received a grammar-school education and were convinced that their background and their speech-idiom had as much right to literary and dramatic expression as those of the middle-class, who had been dominant in both literature and the theatre in Britain for long enough—or so it seemed to them.

Room at the Top 1958. Director Jack Clayton
Laurence Harvey, Heather Sears

A Taste of Honey 1961. Director Tony Richardson
Rita Tushingham, Murray Melvin

It was astonishing to see how the middle-class 'opposition' went down like ninepins, and made a fashionable cult out of a literature of protest which was largely directed against everything they represented. It would seem that the younger middle-class generation (of intellectuals, at least) were as sick of themselves as novels like Kingsley Amis's *Lucky Jim* (1954) so entertainingly implied. This literature of protest recognised quite clearly that the old, polite barriers about what subjects and language were suitable for publication in print or on the stage were an obsolete façade which only needed a concerted push to crumble in a cloud of putrid dust or remain in the form of a picturesque ruin for the young satirists to dismantle brick by brick. It is no coincidence that two notable court cases for the publication of an 'obscene libel' (the first in 1954 concerning Stanley Kauffmann's *The Philanderer* and the second in 1960 concerning the unexpurgated version of D. H. Lawrence's *Lady Chatterley's Lover*) should have spanned this same period. The press, searching as usual for a brand-word, began to call British society 'permissive', implying that 'anything' could now 'go'. In the theatre, the Lord Chamberlain's function as censor (a strange survival from the days when plays could only be performed 'legitimately' in theatres carrying the royal patent) became yet again the subject of direct attack,* while in films the absurdly restrictive policies of the post-war British Board of Film Censors were notably liberalised, though not, of course, abolished altogether.

Whereas in the past a gentleman could always be trusted to know where frankness in mixed company should end and obscene expression confined to male society begin, the working-classes obviously did not—unless, of course, they were highly 'respectable' and sought to 'ape their betters'. *Room at the Top, Saturday Night and Sunday Morning, A Taste of Honey, A Kind of Loving* pulled less and less punches until younger men and women of all classes found themselves talking openly about real-life sex and its perversions, about abortion and contraception, about pornography and obscenity without caring whether they were overheard or not. Fighting something of a rearguard action, censorship of both stage and screen began to back-track, recognising that their function is, as far as possible, to acknowledge what the more responsible members of the greater public are prepared to accept or tolerate on stage or screen, and tailor their prohibitions accordingly.†

* Theatre censorship by the Lord Chamberlain was finally abolished in September 1968.

† The British Board of Film Censors, founded in 1912, acts as an advisory body only, but its categorisation of the films it passes, as well as its outright banning of certain films, are normally accepted by local authorities and their observation imposed on all exhibitors receiving licences to operate cinemas. But the local authorities retain the power to alter or waive the Board's recommendations, and from time to time the London authority, in particular, has done so—a notable recent case being that of the film *Ulysses*, which was specially licensed by London for exhibition. This example was then followed by a very few provincial authorities after the censor had refused to pass it without cuts being made. The special 'X' certificate was introduced by the Board in 1952 in order to permit greater freedom in allowing films to be shown on condition children under sixteen are excluded. The other certificates are 'U' ('universally' open to all age groups) and 'A' (open to children under sixteen only if accompanied by a responsible adult).

As far as the cinema was concerned, the first sign of these new tendencies came in the screen adaptation of *Room at the Top* in 1958. Joe Lampton (Laurence Harvey) knows his welfare state at least enough to take full advantage of it and work his way to the top with cynical energy. His only merit is his frank acknowledgment of his expediency. This working-class Machiavelli appreciates what is 'first-class', and uses sex to get it. His seduction of a magnate's daughter, Susan (Heather Sears), finally secures him wealth at the price of a loveless marriage, and it drives an older woman, who has been his mistress, to suicide. Although this adaptation, Jack Clayton's first major assignment as a director, fell uneasily between an uncompromising exposure of corruption in the relations between Lampton and the rich, cultureless society he aspires to join and a certain novelettishness belonging to an older style in British films, it had an authenticity in its sexual scenes which was new. Laurence Harvey, Simone Signoret and Heather Sears gave exceptionally good performances.

With *Room at the Top* launched and successful, it was the turn of the theatre to contribute the next film—John Osborne's *Look Back in Anger* (1958), adapted for the screen by Nigel Kneale. Osborne contributed the additional dialogue needed for the considerable expansion given to the play, including a new character, 'Ma' Tanner, played by Edith Evans. The dimension of the play was changed; much of Jimmy Porter's diatribes was pruned away. The action was extended outside the stuffy confines of his flat, showing him in relation to other people with whom he establishes quieter, more human relationships, as he does with Ma Tanner. Richard Burton, as always, plays with sincerity, but he appeared far too mature for this part. Only Mary Ure remained from the original stage cast, enduring Jimmy's insults to her class with a silent understanding which amounted to sympathy disguised as insulation from his raging violence. The validity of the play remained in the film, and it represented a strong start for Tony Richardson as a feature director. Along with Osborne, he formed a company, Woodfall, to sponsor films representing the new outlook.

John Osborne himself assisted in the adaptation of his play *The Entertainer* (1960) for Tony Richardson's next film, which was to be one of his best. Again, many of the more revealing interchanges of dialogue were ruthlessly cut to give the film a wider audience appeal; Oswald Morris's vivid in-shooting camerawork

Look Back in Anger 1958. Director Tony Richardson
Richard Burton

thrust the rowdy seaside atmosphere of Morecombe slap on to the screen; the final exposure of the moral, spiritual and professional decline of the bogus entertainer, Archie Rice, occurs against the background of the noisy holidaymakers pushing past the placard proclaiming the Suez crisis in which Archie's only contact with real life, his son Mick, is to die and so break the last shreds of illusion which keep his father going. Richardson used large, oppressive close-ups and shock cutting to the point of technical arrogance, but he brought the audience relentlessly face to face with the failure of the sad characters of Archie and his debilitated, alcoholic wife, beautifully played by Brenda de Banzie. Even though artifice appears at odd moments in the harsh, uncompromising close-ups, Laurence Olivier's performance is an impressive *tour de force*, with his puffy face, glib gestures, flappy restlessness, his sad emptiness of expression in moments of repose. Richardson would not let the audience forget that Archie Rice is a melancholy caricature of themselves; only Archie's daughter, touchingly played by Joan Plowright, offers him a slender lifeline to salvation through her sympathy and compassion.

The Entertainer 1960. Director Tony Richardson
Laurence Olivier, Joan Plowright

Last in the initial series of films which embodied the new style came *Saturday Night and Sunday Morning* (1960), also a Woodfall production. Alan Sillitoe worked on the adaptation of his novel with the director, Karel Reisz, a friend and colleague of Tony Richardson; it was also Reisz's first film as a feature director. The new men were arriving, and *Saturday Night and Sunday Morning* carried the movement, if such it could be called, an appreciable stage forward. Like the other three of these initial films it was given an 'X' certificate. Arthur Seaton (Albert Finney), the young factory worker who is determined to keep his individuality at whatever cost to himself and his girl-friends, has to learn that relationships with other people bring responsibilities. Although he works well and earns good wages, his determination to be independent turns to aggressiveness; he prides himself on his prowess with drink and women. His relationship with Brenda (Rachel Roberts), the wife of a fellow-worker, teaches him what back-street abortion involves; when he transfers his affection to a young unmarried girl, Doreen (Shirley Ann Field), he finds himself faced with the firm prospect of marriage. He learns to accept this responsibility without losing his spirit of independence. This film, with its locations in Nottingham (the city where Sillitoe had himself worked in a bicycle factory) was shot by Freddie Francis, and it had an authenticity which few films since have managed to surpass. Reisz kept the film deliberately quiet, unhistrionic; his people had to be as near as possible recognisably like the majority of those who would be watching it in the cinemas. What was said was like what they would have said in similar circumstances. There was no conventional plot, only a series of events leading to a stage in the development of Arthur's character. This film, which was to be very successful at the box-office, was so exactly observed that no one could escape facing the considerable moral issues involved, though these were left to the audience to resolve.

This particular film owed much to certain documentary and short films which had been made by Reisz, Richardson, Lindsay Anderson and others. *Wakefield Express*, a study of communal life in the West Riding of Yorkshire seen through the work of a group of local newspapers, had been written and directed by Anderson and photographed by Walter Lassally in 1952. The following year Anderson had made a very different film, *O Dreamland*, a corrosive exposure of the primitive 'culture' represented by

Saturday Night and Sunday Morning 1960. Director Karel Reisz
Albert Finney, Rachel Roberts

a South Coast Fun Fair filmed by John Fletcher; and, in association with Guy Brenton, *Thursday's Children*, a deeply sympathetic documentary about the education of deaf-mute children, which was awarded an Oscar. In 1955 *Momma Don't Allow* was made by Karel Reisz and Tony Richardson, and photographed by Walter Lassally among the young people of Wood Green Jazz Club in London. In 1957, with Leon Clore and Karel Reisz as co-producers, and the Ford Motor Company as sponsors, Lindsay Anderson, Walter Lassally and John Fletcher made *Every Day except Christmas*, a film about workers and other people in Covent Garden fruit and vegetable market. Then in 1958 came Karel Reisz's most ambitious film before *Saturday Night and Sunday Morning*, *We are the Lambeth Boys*, a rather self-consciously 'positive' study of the boys in a progressive London youth club made in protest against the current fashionable emphasis on adolescent delinquency.

Most of these films were directly sponsored, but others were assisted by the British Film Institute's Experimental Film Fund, of which Sir Michael Balcon had been Chairman for many years. This fund was first set up in 1952 with a grant of £12,500 from the British Film Production Fund and with, as Balcon put it, 'the aim of encouraging new talent and original ideas in film-making'. This fund in its original form lasted eleven years, until 1963, and after a period of quiescence, was resuscitated as the Film Institute Production Board in 1966, again under the chairmanship of Sir Michael Balcon, with a new grant from government sources. The Fund had assisted around fifty films, and many who were able to realise films they otherwise could never have done were later to become well-known film-makers in feature and shorts production, and producers of films for television. In addition to those already mentioned, the names of Ken Russell, Peter Watkins and Don Levy should be added to those who were later to make feature films in Britain.

These films made in the 1950s contributed to the movement which came to be known as 'free cinema', a term which Reisz and Richardson preferred to 'experimental', with its suggestion of the esoteric. In a manifesto introducing a programme of their work at the National Film Theatre, they wrote: 'In a climate as habitually conventional and free from excitement as that of the British cinema, almost any sign of vitality, or reaction against the norm, would be of note. . . . Like other youthful movements of the moment, in art, in literature, it reflects an increasing concern with the social responsibilities of the artist. . . . These films are free in the sense that their statements are entirely personal . . . No film can be too personal . . . Implicit in our attitude is a belief in freedom, in the importance of people and in the significance of the everyday.'

It was in this spirit that the leading film-makers in the movement had managed at last to penetrate into the world of the commercial feature. When they did so, Tony Richardson, who was also an established stage and television director, was 30 at the time of *Look Back in Anger,* Karel Reisz, who had been born in Czechoslovakia but brought up in England, was 34 when he made *Saturday Night and Sunday Morning,* while Lindsay Anderson, also a noted stage director, was 40 at the time of his first feature film, *This Sporting Life* (1963). For most of them it had been a long time to wait.

Traditional cinema 1958–62

The turning-point in the newer style of British cinema naturally affected only a minority of films. This particular kind of realist cinema, like its counterpart on the stage, was derided by hostile writers as 'kitchen sink' stuff. Naturally enough, once the working-class drama became established as popular in its own right, good, bad and indifferent films were made in its name. But in any case the greater part of British film-making still had little to do with working-class people in a working-class environment. The traditional preoccupations of the cinema—with war, with crime, with sexual excitement—dominated the British screen in terms of the footage exhibited, and among these films were many which for one reason or another have particular interest.

The war films may be represented by several different kinds of film released during this period—*Carve her Name with Pride, Orders to Kill, Ice Cold in Alex* and *Dunkirk* in 1958, *Tunes of Glory* and *Sink the Bismarck!* in 1960, *Guns of Navarone* (1961) and *Zulu* (1963). The first two reconstructed the tensions of service within the French resistance movement. The emphasis in Paul Dehn's script for *Orders to Kill* (director, Anthony Asquith) avoided the surface realities of the so-called documentary approach; far more stylised, it high-lit the psychological pressures on a young man (Paul Massie) sent on a mission to kill an underground agent in France (Leslie French) who is believed to be betraying the Allies. In associating with his essentially gentle victim, the assassin forms the impression that he is innocent. Eventually he is forced by a resolute woman resistance worker (superbly played by Irene Worth) to kill in cold blood the man who had offered him his friendship—a scene which remains in my memory as harshly as the murder of the girl in *Psycho.*

Dunkirk (1958, director Leslie Norman) was one of the last productions of Sir Michael Balcon for Ealing; the famous Ealing Studios had been sold the previous year to BBC television. Determination not to let this film become another flushed and over-heroic battle spectacular, full of meaningless carnage, was not matched by any new creative way of presenting this terrifying

Dunkirk 1958. Director Leslie Norman

example of the wastage of war as well as the everyday heroism of individual people, in or out of uniform, when called on to respond to a crisis. This was a pity—the film had several impressive scenes on the beaches; but the older, sober documentary style was no longer valid. What had once been an effective antidote to the studio histrionics of the past appeared now at times pedestrian. The new factual films had become more personal in observation, more intimate in interpretation.

Ice Cold in Alex (1958) helped establish J. Lee Thompson as an extremely competent director of action films; *Sink the Bismarck!* (1960, produced by John Brabourne and directed by Lewis Gilbert) showed Kenneth More as a rigid disciplinarian in naval operations; he had already shown his capacity for character-acting in the sturdy British image in the part of Douglas Bader in Lewis Gilbert's film *Reach for the Sky* (1956). What was most remarkable about *Sink the Bismarck!* was the technical operation involved in reconstructing the sea-battles in a vast, open-air tank at Pinewood Studios with model aircraft and model ships some twenty feet long. *Tunes of Glory* (1960, director Ronald Neame) represented a shift towards a greater concern with the realities of human relationships, in this case the personal tensions between two disparate commanders in a Highland Regiment—the easy-going, hard-drinking officer played by Alec Guinness and the disciplined, efficient but neurotic man who takes over the command, played by John Mills—showing once again that he had become one of the foremost British actors.

In *Guns of Navarone* (1959–61, directed by J. Lee Thompson, with a cast led by Gregory Peck, David Niven and Anthony Quinn), the American producer-screenwriter Carl Foreman made his greatest bid so far in British production as the writer-producer of a high-budgeted spectacular war film. A small commando unit is sent on a seemingly impossible mission to relieve a British force besieged on an island off Turkey by putting the twin German monster-guns of Navarone out of action. Relationships became a crucial part of the film—the degree of ruthlessness required for responsible leadership—and to some extent this came in conflict with the varied excitements of the action. The intentions of *Guns of Navarone* were serious, if somewhat confusing, and the sheer scale of the production and its high cost represented a new, Americanised element in British film-making of the period. Finally *Zulu* (director Cy Endfield) took its subject from a barely remembered campaign in 1879 in Natal, and was memorable for the fine deployment of its panoramic battle-scenes. It was also Stanley Baker's first film as a producer as well as a star.

The large-scale kind of production, given popular support and wide international distribution, has always been one of the surest investments in success known in the cinema—no other form of entertainment (and certainly not television) can rival it on the blown-up screens of the larger theatres. An unmatched story of success in these bigger productions was to be the combined work of Sam Spiegel and David Lean starting with *The Bridge on the River Kwai* (1957, originally scripted by Pierre Boulle from his novel, with additional, but uncredited, scripting by

The Bridge on the River Kwai 1957. Director David Lean
Sessue Hayakawa, Alec Guinness

Carl Foreman), which by 1959 had been seen by some 235 million people throughout the world. It contained another of Alec Guinness's feats of acting as Colonel Nicolson, the obsessed officer who, as a prisoner of war, builds a bridge for the Japanese which becomes so much the apple of his eye that he forgets he is serving the enemy by keeping the morale of his men high through this work of construction. Nicolson is at once absurd and admirable, his fine moral stand made a nonsense by the inhumane logic of war. The irony of the film was somewhat lost in the visual beauty of the locations in Ceylon (shot under the supervision of Jack Hillyard) and the 'heroics' of the treatment, and the end (when Nicolson himself destroys the bridge by falling on the detonator after being killed) avoids the central issue raised by the film. However, the large profits made were reinvested in the even more ambitious production of *Lawrence of Arabia* (1962, scripted by Robert Bolt, co-produced by Spiegel and Lean, who directed), with Peter O'Toole as Lawrence and Jack Hawkins as Allenby. This film represented in all some four years' work, and is reputed to have cost four million pounds. Photographed by Freddie Young almost entirely on locations in Jordan, Morocco and Spain (where buildings in Seville were adapted by the art director, John Box, to represent mansions in the Middle East), this film was first of all a major technical triumph of cinematography; the desert, heat shimmer, mirages and all, has never been filmed so superbly. The interpretation of Lawrence's character, with its fascist undertones, roused some public controversy.*

Carol Reed, who produced and directed *Our Man in Havana* (1959), once more worked with a brilliant script from Graham Greene; the film helped feed the perennial interest in the profession of the spy while at the same time satirising its basic amorality. Alec Guinness turned the diminutive Wormold into an enthusiast inventing revelations with all the mastery of an amateur of genius, and extracting himself adroitly when real trouble begins so that he receives an inevitable OBE. The film had a beautiful visual polish, the combined work of the designer John Box and

* A special issue of the *Journal of the Society of Film and Television Arts*, Winter 1962–3, gives a full account of the conception and production of this film.

Lawrence of Arabia 1962. Director David Lean
Peter O'Toole, Omar Sharif

the photographic director Oswald Morris. Carol Reed's assured, professional direction sustained the difficult balance between comedy and terror.

A light touch of satire characterised several films of this period —for example, the comedies featuring Peter Sellers, *I'm All Right, Jack* (1959, director and co-scriptwriter John Boulting) and *Only Two Can Play* (1961, scripted by Bryan Forbes from Kingsley Amis's novel, *That Uncertain Feeling,* and directed by Sidney

I'm All Right, Jack 1959. Director John Boulting
Margaret Rutherford

Gilliat). The first of these received some rather over-earnest criticism, alleging that it was merely facetious in dealing with irresponsible, work-shy strikers and dishonest employers, but Peter Sellers, Irene Handl and Margaret Rutherford in fact produced beautifully-observed performances, well above caricature. John and Roy Boulting had already begun their succession of what appear now as mildly satiric comedies, with *Brothers-in-Law* (1956) and *Lucky Jim* (1957), both featuring Ian Carmichael.

Brothers-in-Law 1956. Director Roy Boulting
Ian Carmichael, Richard Attenborough

Only Two Can Play was somewhat more conventional, but the experimental, easily-punctured love affair played by Peter Sellers and Mai Zetterling had more genuine comedy than the rest of the film.

By now Bryan Forbes, an actor who had turned increasingly to screenwriting, was also establishing himself as both producer and director, working in association with Richard Attenborough. Among his earlier films were *The Angry Silence* (1960, director Guy Green) which he scripted and co-produced, and which featured Richard Attenborough, and *Whistle Down the Wind* (1961), which he co-produced and directed. (The adaptation from the story by Mary Hayley Bell was made, incidentally, by Keith Waterhouse and Willis Hall—who were to become one of the most prolific writing teams of the 1960s for theatre, film and television, their earlier screenplays including *Billy Liar* and *A Kind of Loving*). *The Angry Silence* was a genuine attempt to give dramatic life to industrial problems; the central character,

The Angry Silence 1960. Director Guy Green
Richard Attenborough

Only Two Can Play 1961. Director Sidney Gilliat
Graham Stark, Peter Sellers, Mai Zetterling

a worker played by Richard Attenborough, asserts his individual right to dissent from strike action, in spite of the violence done to himself and his child as a result of mob-rule masquerading as trade unionism. Credit is due for making this film at all, and for the forthrightness of much of its dialogue. There had been almost nothing on the British screen about abuses within the trade unions, though Bernard Miles's *Chance of a Lifetime* should not be overlooked, nor, for comparison and contrast, Elia Kazan's American film, *On the Waterfront* (1954). *Whistle Down the Wind,* Bryan Forbes's first attempt at direction, with Hayley Mills, Alan Bates and Bernard Lee, was a somewhat over-symbolised but touching and largely unsentimental study of a group of country children, beautifully played, who believe an escaped prisoner whom they find injured in a barn to be Jesus of the Sunday-school come back again to earth. Bryan Forbes's more recent films will be referred to later.

Term of Trial (1962, scripted and directed by the stage producer, Peter Glenville) was an altogether darker film about the effects of children on adult relationships; it was slow, loaded, oppressive and remarkable mainly for Laurence Olivier's quietude and the first appearance of Sarah Miles and Terence Stamp (who had, however, already played the completely divergent part of Billy Budd in Peter Ustinov's impressive film which was to be released shortly afterwards).

After the airing given to the subject of censorship during the controversy about *Spare the Rod,* another film of delinquency in schools (1961, director Leslie Norman), the censorship of 'X' certificated films began to relax still further in tune with the growing acceptance of hitherto 'difficult' material by the general public. In this relaxation of former tensions in censorship, the contribution of BBC television drama was of great significance. It was the Canadian, Sidney Newman, who was head of BBC television drama from 1963–7, who brought an entirely new

Term of Trial 1962. Director Peter Glenville
Laurence Olivier, Simone Signoret

drive into the search for new producers, writers, directors and actors, and who literally trained his audience of millions to accept drama which not only explored human and social relationships in unconventional ways, but gradually introduced new screen techniques to do so. He had begun his career as a film-maker with John Grierson at the National Film Board of Canada during the war, and before moving over to the BBC he had been in charge of ABC television drama and producer of its Armchair Theatre from 1958. Bold experiments were frequently undertaken at ABC by his writers, who included Alun Owen, Harold Pinter, Ted Willis and Jane Arden, and his directors, Philip Saville, Ted Kotcheff and Alvin Rakoff.

As we shall see shortly, television was to provide a great deal of new talent for British films, more especially in the mid-1960s. But at this stage we are concerned with the changing attitudes to subject and treatment which a more relaxed censorship permitted. Sidney Newman's men and women sensed the changing public mood and, in their best work, educated the public to face the realities of our time. Writing in 1964, Sidney Newman said: 'Writers must help here too. They must force themselves to regard as urgent the problems of winning and holding the big audience—to find the significant themes or old themes demonstrated in sharp contemporary terms . . . They must add to their present reasonably realistic studio approach greater believability by getting their electronic cameras and videotape units out on location, and, secondly, ridding themselves of most naturalistic trappings . . . I am thinking of the totally unnaturalistic play—a dramatic shorthand. The kind of production where a good story is told in a kind of Fellini way . . . A story where all the irrelevancies are eliminated, where we move from place to place by the simple and glorious act of the cut without the in-between fol-de-rol of getting there . . . We need to be aware that plays are more than trivial entertainment, that we must help our writers to have trust in their own ability to interpret their age.'*

It was, after all, more or less the same public who were providing audiences of six to ten million or more for the plays of David Mercer or Harold Pinter on BBC and ITV television, who were ready to respond to the changes taking place outside their homes in the cinema.

**Journal of the Society of Film and Television Arts,* Spring 1964.

Regional accents 1960–4

The mass of plays on television using the working-class idiom set in the various regions of Britain with a proudly indigenous tradition were soon matched in the cinema by the successors to *Saturday Night and Sunday Morning.* Tony Richardson produced and directed *A Taste of Honey* (1961, adapted and expanded from her play by Shelagh Delaney in association with Tony Richardson) and *The Loneliness of the Long-Distance Runner* (1962, script by Alan Sillitoe from his short story); both owed much to Walter Lassally's photography and Ralph Brinton's ability to make viable sets out of actual buildings on locations. *A Taste of Honey* stands out as one of Richardson's successes; authentic, touching, seldom marred by technical excesses, it owes its primary richness to the intimate yet strongly characterised acting of Rita Tushingham, with her beautiful pointed features and wide eyes, and by Murray Melvin (from Joan Littlewood's Theatre Workshop) as the young homosexual who looks after the unmarried girl when she is pregnant. *The Loneliness of the Long-Distance Runner* was the first film in which Tom Courtenay came to star rank, though he had appeared the same year in an effective, modest-budget film, *Private Potter* (director, Casper Wrede). In both he played the under-privileged boy who cannot, or will not, adjust himself to society's established codes—in Private Potter's case, the combined weight of the officer-caste, backed by psychiatrist and padre; in the Borstal boy Colin Smith's case, the antagonisms of a selfish older generation at home and, once he is in trouble, the rigours of discipline and gamesmanship at a Borstal under a Governor steeped in the British public school tradition. In no film has Tony Richardson seemed more in debt to outside influences of style than in this case, with its complex, multiple flashbacks and self-indulgent technique obscuring to a considerable extent Tom Courtenay's performance, and the significance of his struggle with the Governor (Michael Redgrave). This was a struggle parallel in many ways to that in *Saturday Night and Sunday Morning,* for there too a potentially valuable human spirit with an admirable quality of independence is wasted in determined, fruitless opposition to the social establishment.

Another director, John Schlesinger, was to come from documentary film-making, mainly for television. His first feature film, after he had won substantial awards for his documentary *Terminus,* was *A Kind of Loving* (1962, scripted by Keith Waterhouse and Willis Hall from Stan Barstow's novel), with Alan Bates and June Ritchie. This film dealt openly with youthful sex relations and the social snobbishness which exists in working-

The Loneliness of the Long Distance Runner 1962. Director Tony Richardson
Tom Courtenay

A Kind of Loving 1962. Director John Schlesinger
Alan Bates, June Ritchie

Lunn's

class society. Its success led to Schlesinger's next film, *Billy Liar* (1963), which Waterhouse and Hall adapted from their own play; Tom Courtenay as Billy showed his capacity for sympathetic comedy and his skill in stretches of improvised acting. The film itself was rich in comic characterisation and comic episodes, such as the opening of a new self-service store; it also introduced Julie Christie in the part of a free-living, nomadic girl who cheerfully picks up work, and men, where she wants.

Lindsay Anderson's *This Sporting Life* (1963) carried the British cinema a stage forward in the treatment of both situation and character. Shot on location in Wakefield, the film was not merely a realist study of a Rugby player; as Anderson himself put it: 'The film is primarily a study of temperament. It is a film about a man of extraordinary power and aggressiveness, both temperamental and physical, but at the same time with a great innate sensitiveness and a need for love of which he is at first hardly aware. And this sensitiveness is reflected in a very strange and

Billy Liar 1963. Director John Schlesinger
Julie Christie

This Sporting Life 1963. Director Lindsay Anderson
Richard Harris, Rachel Roberts

complicated relationship with a woman . . . We were very aware that we were not making a film about anything representative; we were making a film about something unique . . . about an extraordinary (and therefore more deeply significant) man, and about an extraordinary relationship.'

Richard Harris as Machin, the Rugby player, created an uneasy bear of a man lodging with Mrs Hammond (Rachel Roberts), a widow inhibited by memories of a dead husband whom she loved with a destructive possessiveness. They become involved in an unsatisfying love affair which neither of them know how to develop into something positive. Machin leaves mining and turns professional on the football field as a gesture, partly to impress the woman and partly because this is the only way he knows how to establish his identity in the world and gain recognition. The film is told in a succession of flashbacks; Machin is given gas by a dentist following an accident on the field, and as a result he recalls the stages of his unstable, at times rebellious relationship with his fellow players, with the unscrupulous promoters of the team, and above all with Mrs Hammond. The game itself, which opens the film at the time of the accident, is shown like a struggle of gladiators, our contemporary titans—for as Machin says himself, the team represents for the town the spirit of action and heroism which the crowd as individuals can no longer live up to in their own lives. The film ends with stark tragedy when the woman dies and Machin is left to discover in mute mourning that the need for love went far deeper than he was ever able to realise when she was alive.

Richardson, Schlesinger and Anderson liked to work as far as possible away from studios. For example, Schlesinger has said: 'My main objection to working in a studio is that you tend to get a factory atmosphere, and you are forced to blueprint the work in advance. So I must say I prefer taking a unit away from a studio and working in a manner which needn't be in every single respect predetermined. Besides, I like bringing in real people who live in the area where I'm working. I don't think a studio necessarily gives your technicians more freedom, whereas skilled technicians working on location do have a very real freedom. This, as I see it, is why the Woodfall people prefer to work away from a studio.'*

Other directors were to make working-class subjects. Ian Hendry and June Ritchie played the leads in *Live Now, Pay Later*

* *SFTA Journal*, Spring 1963, 'The New Realism in British Films'.

(1962, director Jay Lewis), a sharply satirical comedy, with a touch of melodrama, about the evils of pressurised salesmanship in hire-purchased goods. Clive Donner, using locations in Bristol, made *Some People* (1962), which featured Kenneth More as an understanding church organist trying to help a frustrated group of teenage guitarists whom authority merely regard as dangerous nuisances with their high-speed motor-bikes; one of the lesser parts was played by David Hemmings. Sidney J. Furie's *The Leather Boys* (1963) made a stronger impact with its splendid naturalistic playing using partially improvised dialogue; Dot (Rita Tushingham) faces the breakdown of her youthful marriage because of her husband's attraction for a boyfriend with homosexual

On pages 72/73
Half-a-Sixpence 1967. Director George Sidney
Tommy Steele

The Leather Boys 1963. Director Sidney J. Furie
Dudley Sutton, Colin Campbell

tendencies; both young men are motor-bike enthusiasts. Only the homosexual gathering at the close of the film became weak and theatrical. Joan Littlewood's incursion into film-making, *Sparrows Can't Sing* (1963) resulted in a lively, attractive Cockney comedy.

The initial freshness of the working-class film was later debased by films introducing standardised music-hall caricature and low farce, or turning into sentimental cliché the dangerous subject of youthful delinquency in which everyone is wrong but the delinquent. One of the pleasanter forms the movement took, however, was to produce a few modest attempts at musicals, the most successful of which was Sidney J. Furie's *The Young Ones* (1961) with Cliff Richard. Other attempts at producing a British teenage musical form from original material were not so successful, and the highly-budgeted Anglo-American film version of *Half-a-Sixpence* (1967) directed by George Sidney with Tommy Steele's skilled and effervescent performance owes far more to Hollywood's out-and-out professionalism than to any British tradition in this form. More immediately indigenous was Wolf Mankowicz's astringent but engaging musical *Expresso Bongo* (1960), directed by Val Guest.

Sparrows Can't Sing 1963. Director Joan Littlewood
James Booth Roy Kinnear, Bryan Murphy,

Later, with censorship receding still further in the matter of sexual situations and references, came the ironic comedies *Alfie* (1966, director Lewis Gilbert, with Michael Caine) and *Here We Go Round the Mulberry Bush* (1967, Clive Donner). Donner's ruthlessly modish comic melodrama, *Nothing But the Best*, had appeared in 1964, scripted by Frederic Raphael, with an excellent performance by Alan Bates as a young man on the make. *Here We Go Round the Mulberry Bush* was set in Stevenage New Town, its decorative modern piazza and less decorative road-side pave-

Alfie 1966. Director Lewis Gilbert
Michael Caine, Millicent Martin

ments thronging with youngsters taking preliminary examinations in sex. It is true that the film, derived from a story by Hunter Davies, pokes fun at all this time-consuming activity, and centres on the chronic inexperience of Jamie, a comely and cheerful schoolboy of seventeen who can only day-dream about sex instead of 'having it off', as all his companions boast they are doing. He comes from a prosperous working-class home, where the weekly religious ritual consists in filling up and checking football pools. Jamie's daydreams are what give this film its

Here We Go Round the Mulberry Bush 1967. Director Clive Donner
Barry Evans

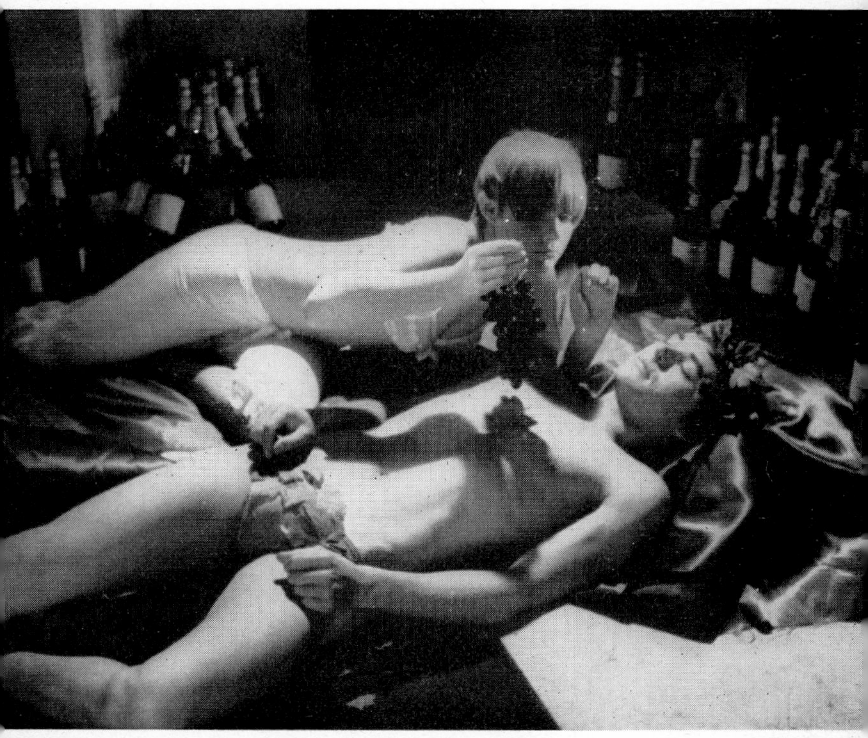

style, or multiplicity of styles, since they break out into all kinds of forms from silent film burlesque to parodies of various contemporary 'X'-type films which fill the bursting imagination of a boy who at seventeen has had the right to see them for quite a while. The film was immensely, brashly entertaining, though the dialogue seemed more self-consciously literate than authentic.

Alfie was also, to some extent, burlesque. It showed the youthful East-End Londoner whose ceaseless pursuit of girls (played by a unique range of celebrities, including Shelley Winters,

Nothing but the Best 1964. Director Clive Donner
Millicent Martin

Millicent Martin, Vivien Merchant, Shirley Ann Field and Eleanor Bron) finally catches him out. He develops a fondness for the baby produced by one of the girls, and when another of his children by a married woman is stillborn, he receives a final shock of self-recognition. This film (with a script by Bill Naughton from his own play) lacked the psychological sensitivity it might have had, and was in consequence played too hard for laughs. Another of Bill Naughton's plays, *The Family Way* (1966), was adapted sympathetically for the screen by the Boultings.

The Family Way 1966. Director Roy Boulting
Hayley Mills

Outside tradition

All films are prototypes and must stand or fall individually with the public. But most films reduce this risk as far as possible by presenting themselves as recognisably like other films which have proved successful. But in addition to the films by Tony Richardson, Karel Reisz and others which were creating new precedents, there were a number which cannot be easily categorised and to a lesser or greater extent took the box-office risk of being unusual. *The Horse's Mouth* (1959, directed by Ronald Neame) was adapted by Alec Guinness from Joyce Cary's novel and gave this great actor an eccentric, difficult part of his own choice as Gulley Jimson, Cary's vagrant artist, whose genius constantly erupts through his irresponsible, vagabond nature. This per-

The Horse's Mouth 1959. Director Ronald Neame
Alec Guinness

Peeping Tom 1959. Director Michael Powell
Anna Massey, Karl Heinz Boehm

formance was at the very least notable, though both the film and the conception of Jimson lacked the full richness of Cary's anarchic characterisation. Other films which followed broke the fatal stereotypes of the cinema—*Peeping Tom* (1959), *Victim* (1961) and *Lord of the Flies* (1961–3), a film the circuit exhibitors rejected until they saw the success it enjoyed through specialised release in 1964.

Michael Powell's remarkable film *Peeping Tom* was derived in certain respects from de Sade and anticipated in others the kind of appallingly sadistic experiments revealed in the Moors case of

1966. Like *Blow-Up* seven years later, photography became an integral part of the action of this film, since the leading character, a pathological murderer, specialises in filming the deaths of his victims. He has become what he is because his father has used him as a child for experiments in the inducement of fear, recording his screams for subsequent study. The film, presented as a psychological thriller, revolted some critics, and it certainly contained melodramatic elements which at times vitiated its psychological interest and its technical ingenuity. Had it been released a few years later, and treated as a serious film rather than a 'shocker', it might have been received differently. Certainly, abnormal psychology should never be exploited for thrills; but this film is in the same class as *Repulsion* in its stark dramatisation of abnormality, and this may account for the censor's apparent leniency in allowing it exhibition in 1959.

In 1961 Michael Relph and Basil Dearden made *Victim*, one of the earliest specific studies of the homosexual and his vulnerability to blackmail before the recent law reforms. The key scriptwriter was Janet Green, who had already worked on *Sapphire* (1959). The result, though to some extent presented as conventional screen drama, was a remarkably sensitive film; Dirk Bogarde was outstanding as a barrister, with strong but repressed homosexual tendencies, who risks his career and his marriage in his determination to track down a group of blackmailers. The film was explicit in its handling of the problem of the homosexual, and its release marked once again a step forward in a progressive censorship policy.

Another film of psychological interest was Peter Brook's adaptation of William Golding's *Lord of the Flies*, a fable about the kind of social psychological regression a community of very young boys might suffer if isolated on a desert island for some years without adults. In spite of the attempts at civilised leadership by Ralph, who is twelve, and the short-sighted, asthmatic Piggy, who can talk and has a mind of his own, the boys who are mostly ten years of age or even younger decline into instinctual savagery under the influence of Jack, the destructive bully with a talent for hunting and killing. The boys chosen by Peter Brook were taken to live on an island off Puerto Rico, and submitted to the gruelling experience of making real the truth of Golding's fable. The story was shot in the strict order of the narrative, while in addition Brook kept the camera as free as possible to catch

Lord of the Flies 1961–3. Director Peter Brook

every significant moment of improvisation the children devised. Their looks reflected this darkening experience far more than their voices, and much of the dialogue (spoken in a deadening middle-class English) had to be said without the child actor's face in direct vision. The film presents an experience more than a story.

In 1963 the experiment was made by Lord Birkett and Clive Donner of filming Harold Pinter's successful play *The Caretaker,* using two of the original cast from the theatre (Alan Bates and Donald Pleasence) and a location largely confined to the attic of an empty house in Hackney. The budget was set deliberately low (some £30,000) so that a specialised release might suffice. The great talent of Pinter as a dramatist had been first revealed fully on television, and in most of his earlier plays he takes a close look at a small group of characters locked up in a world which seems to lie on the borderline of insanity. It is Pinter's particular distinction as a writer that he can reveal the tragi-comedy of the whole human condition in the enclosed, obsessional experience of the sub-normal or the paranoiac. In *The Caretaker,* Davies, the tramp who seeks recognition as an individual, is alternately arrogant, frustrated or whining; he is betrayed by his illusions, yet clings to his remnants of human dignity. The presence of this stranger in the house excites a sadistic jealousy in Mick, the younger of the two brothers with whom he is staying, but to each of these three men the crowded attic where they sleep surrounded by piles of useless junk becomes a refuge from the cold world of reality outside. Donald Pleasence's performance as Davies, seen in the continual close-shot of Nicholas Roeg's camera imposed by the attic location, is a savage experience. Michael Birkett has said: 'A set may prove to be more evocative for a certain scene than any location you could find. Contrarywise, a location may prove to have more fantasy about it than the most fantastical studio set . . . The finest directors and technicians often do much of their best work in the most adverse conditions. Sometimes the limitations of a tiny room on location dictate ways of shooting which are more imaginative and more evocative than what would have transpired on a comfortable, well-rigged, all-floating set.'*

* *SFTA Journal,* Spring 1963.

The Caretaker 1963. Director Clive Donner
Donald Pleasence

Pinter went on to write the script for *The Pumkin Eater* (1964), adapted from Penelope Mortimer's novel about Jo, a woman who, although a compulsive child-bearer, cannot keep her men. Her present husband (played by Peter Finch) is a screenwriter called Jake, who loves her but cannot help toying with infidelity. As written by Penelope Mortimer, this story takes the form of Jo's sardonic revelation of her life and its fantasies; the novel has a basic humour as well as a compelling pathology about it. As a film, *The Pumpkin Eater* becomes objective, technically elegant, beautifully directed by Jack Clayton, but cold, only now and then allowing the raw emotion of this woman to show. Peter Finch plays Jake with that particular kind of insensitive charm and off-hand bad manners which turns the character into everywoman's pet. Anne Bancroft plays Jo with all the vigorous virtuosity of which she is capable. But for all its hardness, *The Pumpkin Eater* is a strong and unusual film. Its successor, *Our Mother's House* (1967, with Dirk Bogarde) in which a family of mother-obsessed children manage to secrete her dead body in a woodshed and create a ritual in memory of her, was well directed and acted by the children, but proved too contrived a situation to be dramatically or psychologically acceptable.

More delicate as a study of obsessive love was another film of 1964, adapted by Edna O'Brien from her novel *The Lonely Girl.* This was *The Girl with Green Eyes,* and showed the devotion of a young Irish country-girl (Rita Tushingham) for a middle-aged writer (Peter Finch) living in Dublin. Produced by Tony Richardson, this was the first film as director made by the cinematographer, Desmond Davis, and it was (apart from some over-smart cutting here and there) a sensitive and beautifully acted film, with an amusing supporting performance by Lynn Redgrave. Davis's next film, *The Uncle* (1965) still remains, most unfortunately, unseen in Britain while *I Was Happy Here* (1966) was another love-story, simple, perhaps over-simple, but sincere.

Many of Ken Annakin's most recent films have been American productions but *Those Magnificent Men in their Flying Machines* (1965) was British and made such spectacular use of veteran airplanes that they quite eclipsed an international cast of players.

On pages 88/89
The Pumpkin Eater 1964. Director Jack Clayton
Anne Bancroft

Girl with Green Eyes 1964. Director Desmond Davis
Lynn Redgrave, Rita Tushingham

Seance on a Wet Afternoon (1964) and *The Whisperers* (1967) reveal the maturity of Bryan Forbes's talent as both writer and director. Both films offer superb parts for actresses capable of playing women whose minds are unbalanced. The first concerns a professional medium (played by the American actress, Kim Stanley) whose desire for recognition takes the form of persuading her husband (Richard Attenborough) to abduct a child so that she may 'divine' its whereabouts. The second is a study of a poverty-stricken old-age pensioner (Edith Evans) with pathetic delusions of grandeur. As a writer, Bryan Forbes has an admirable sense of dialogue; as a director, he has an equally admirable sense of how to get the best out of actors. His films, which often edge near melodrama and sentimentality, always allow for subtlety and an unhurried exploration of human feeling.

The Whisperers 1967. Director Bryan Forbes
Edith Evans

Seance on a Wet Afternoon 1964. Director Bryan Forbes
Kim Stanley, Richard Attenborough

Tony Richardson made *Tom Jones* in 1963 and was to complete (after directing two much-criticised films with Jeanne Moreau, *Sailor from Gibraltar* and *Mademoiselle*; and also *The Loved One* in the U.S.A.) *The Charge of the Light Brigade* (1968). John Osborne adapted Fielding's novel for the first, and was initially involved in the scripting of the second, which was finally entrusted to Charles Wood. Faithful to his love for authentic locations, Richardson shot *Tom Jones* mainly in Dorset and Somerset at Nettlecombe Court and in Cerne Abbas, as well as in London. 'By giving the film a completely true physical *look*, I have been able to be free cinematically,' said Richardson in a *Life* interview. 'I have shot it all as if it were happening today. I am a director of improvisation.' The result (photographed by Walter Lassally and Desmond Davis) was fresh and uninhibited, though invaded now and then by such cinematic jokes as freezing a shot or speeding up the action. One brilliantly handled sequence, the *tour de force* of the stag hunt, was a bloody exposure of the cruelty of the chase. The cast, led by Albert Finney, Hugh Griffith, Edith Evans and Susannah York, entered into the spirit of this elaborate, eighteenth-century romp.

Richardson's production, four years later, of *The Charge of the Light Brigade*, was on a much larger scale with a budget of some two million pounds. Shot mainly on location in Turkey, with the help of the Turkish cavalry, the climax of the film, the charge itself, had a visual beauty and horror which came from the combined talents of Richardson, his director of photography, David Watkin, and his editor, Kevin Brownlow, whose own television film of homage to the French director Abel Gance appeared shortly afterwards. Gance's phantasmagoric fast cutting on the battlefields in his pioneer widescreen film *Napoleon* (1926) seems reflected at times in Richardson's film. The characterisation of the principals, Raglan by John Gielgud, Cardigan by Trevor Howard, Lucan by Harry Andrews, is never in terms of conventional spectacle-film simplicity; rather it verges on Hogarthian caricature, making these men monstrous survivals of eighteenth-century self-indulgence at the expense of the common man who dies in dirt and blood in order to sustain their pride. That punitive satire rather than historical exactitude was the policy of the film was reinforced by Richard Williams's invigorating cartoon sequences which punctuated the political and warfare sequences with animated versions of engravings from *Punch* and the

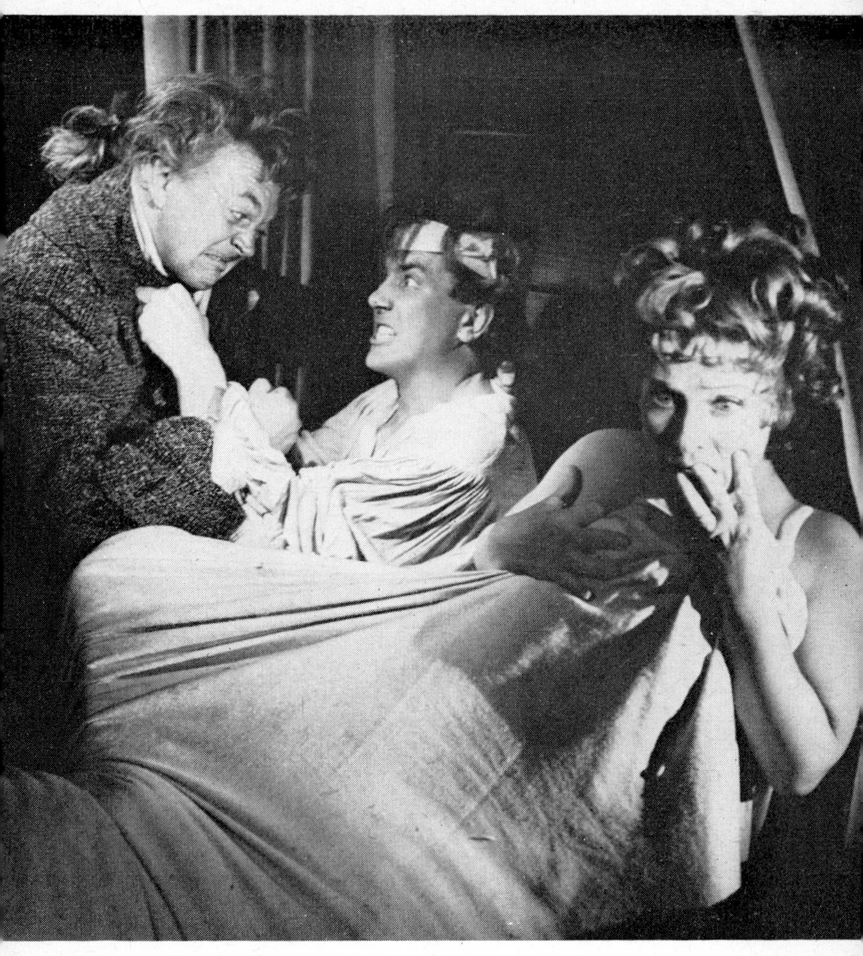

Tom Jones 1963. Director Tony Richardson
Albert Finney, Joyce Redman, George A. Cooper

On pages 94/95

The Charge of the Light Brigade 1968. Director Tony Richardson
Alan Dobie

Illustrated London News of the period. This impressive film suffered from a lack of artistic unity, mixing realism with satiric stylisation which pushed the comedy at times to the point of farce.

John Schlesinger's films, after *A Kind of Loving* and *Billy Liar,* were *Darling* (1965) and *Far From the Madding Crowd* (1967); both were scripted by Frederic Raphael (the first being an original screenplay), and both featured Julie Christie. Diana, the 'darling' of the title, is an example of infantile sophistication on the make;

Far From the Madding Crowd 1967. Director John Schlesinger
Julie Christie, Terence Stamp

Darling 1965. Director John Schlesinger
Julie Christie, Dirk Bogarde

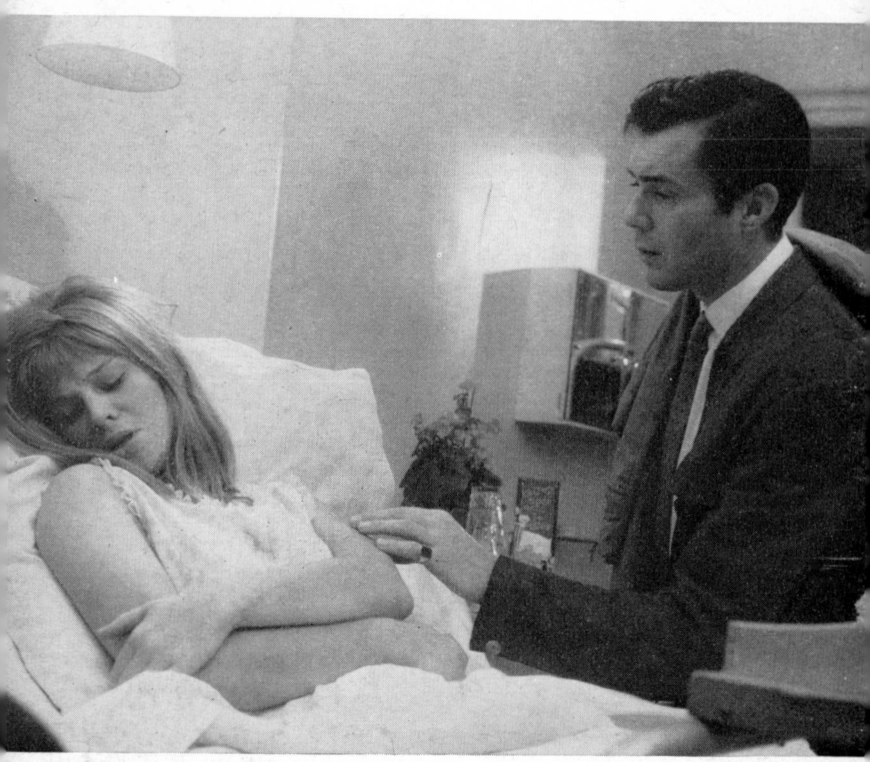

she is a cover-girl who breaks up the marriage of a serious-minded television interviewer (Dirk Bogarde), gets into films with the help of a perverted sales executive, and ends up as the bored wife of an ageing Italian prince. The real intention of this film, exposure of the compulsive narcissism of our time, is to some extent diverted; *Darling* becomes a form of skilful voyeurism, watching the vicious behaviour of shallow, would-be sophisticated people. The film is always in danger of becoming a glossy entertainment without that hard core of strong feeling that makes true satire bite home. Julie Christie, one of the warmest, most human of our younger actresses, fought hard to make this awful girl as human as herself. Her reward was both an Oscar and a British Film Academy Award. She is much more sympathetic, more genuine in *Far From the Madding Crowd*, though less in stature and significance than Hardy's Bathsheba and with too little sense of period. The film proved more conventional in its treatment of Hardy than one had hoped, though beautifully photographed in colour by Nicholas Roeg with magnificent landscapes. The most remarkable sequence was that when Bathsheba endures Sergeant Troy's sadistic swordplay, but only Peter Finch reached out towards the high, dour passions of Hardy's characterisation.

Another fashionably dark comedy-melodrama with a very similar outlook to *Darling* in its exposure of the sickness in our society (while at the same time ruthlessly squeezing it for the maximum dramatic entertainment) was Michael Winner's *I'll Never Forget What's 'is Name* (1967). Films such as this, and *Nothing But the Best* or *Darling* (and in its own particular way, *Blow-Up*) caught the contemporary mood of cynical self-hatred which underlies the success-stories of people with marked ability who prostitute their talents in the shadier areas of show business and advertising. It paid to swing with swinging London even if it made you feel sick.

It was to Karel Reisz, and the dramatist David Mercer, that credit must go for achieving (with the far-seeing help of their producer, Leon Clore) the most unusual British film to gain a wide popular success—*Morgan, a Suitable Case for Treatment* (1966). It would seem to be entirely out of step with the normal box-office film; it is intensely funny about serious matters, and it weaves in and

I'll Never Forget What's 'is Name 1967. Director Michael Winner
Orson Welles

out of fantasy following Morgan's own demented responses. Morgan was David Warner's first major part in a film; he gives this young, working-class artist just the right combination of utter impossibility and deep sympathy, so that Leonie, his 'deb' wife's continued feeling for him as she fights for a 'sensible' divorce can be understood. Vanessa Redgrave's Leonie is a perfect match for this demanding situation. The film is at once wildly hilarious and very sad, and its success, like that of *Blow-Up*, showed that contemporary audiences will support the unclassifiable, off-beat film if it is sufficiently diverting and well-made. Karel Reisz's next film was *Isadora* (1968) with Vanessa Redgrave as Isadora Duncan.

Albert Finney made a brilliant debut as a director with *Charlie Bubbles* (1968, script by Shelagh Delaney). This was the story of a successful writer from the north whose insulated, money-laden life has only served to destroy his human relationships. The film

Isadora 1968. Director Karel Reisz
Vanessa Redgrave

Morgan, a Suitable Case for Treatment 1966. Director Karel Reisz
David Warner

King and Country 1964. Director Joseph Losey
Tom Courtenay, Vivian Matalon

On pages 104/105
The Servant 1963. Director Joseph Losey
James Fox, Dirk Bogarde

was constructed with an economy which can only be called daring for a British film; its restraint was almost painful in its observation of quiet unhappiness as portrayed by Albert Finney himself and, especially, by Billie Whitelaw as the writer's estranged wife.

No director has fought more consistently to make films with a strong individual style and significance than Joseph Losey, the American director and screenwriter who came to work in Britain in 1952 during the period of the McCarthy hearings in the United States. Since that time his films have been made principally in Britain. In America he had the advantage of working also in the theatre, and of collaborating with Berthold Brecht, to whom he acknowledges a great debt. Losey is essentially an analytical director, subjecting his work to prolonged self-criticism. This innate honesty makes him very aware of failure, or partial failure, and the results of this can be seen in the interviews he has recorded with Tom Milne for the book, *Losey on Losey*. His films, both American and British, are almost entirely concerned either with violence in modern society or with difficult sexual relationships, sometimes with both. As his films have deepened and become more complex, he has tried to draw away from the simpler 'realism' of such action pictures as *The Criminal* (1960) to forms which reveal a situation rather than merely relate it. From this standpoint he feels he has achieved much more in the full (not the mutilated) version of *Eve* (1962), and in films such as *King and Country* (1964), *The Servant* (1963) and *Accident* (1967), in which human relationships are of much greater importance than plot, though plot-development is never absent from Losey's films.

Losey's consciousness of the social involvement of the artist has grown with the years—from a comparatively simple, leftist viewpoint to one of much maturer complexity. 'You can only provide a stimulation which I think at its best is some sort of complete artistic statement, which therefore is form and emotion, which will stimulate the people seeing, hearing, absorbing it, to further thought and investigation. Which is why things certainly should have many different levels, and why many interpretations of films, if they're that good, are perfectly justified, even though they may not be fully intended by the creators or fully thought out by them.'* His films have certainly excited this diverse comment. He regards himself now as a 'romantic . . . an emotional sucker' who enjoys working, for example, with Pinter, 'because he is a poet'.

Maturity has meant a movement away from the obvious kind of realistic action which the cinema in its more superficial form can present with such force and fluency. 'I want to move further and further away from explorations of the culmination of this immediate reality impact into less directly realistic and less literal aspects of film. A few people are beginning to do this, but the explorations have hardly started . . . Resnais is a pioneer, and in a quite different way, Godard also.' Losey has therefore become extremely conscious of technical nuances—of photographic and

* All quotations from *Losey on Losey*, edited by Tom Milne, Secker and Warburg (1967).

The Damned 1962. Director Joseph Losey
Viveca Lindfors, Oliver Reed

aural implications; there are many detailed examples discussed in his book. From these considerations have emerged the 'density' of *The Servant* (with Dirk Bogarde, James Fox and Sarah Miles), with its horrifying, Faust-like situation of the gradual invasion of the 'normal' personality of the 'master' by the 'abnormal', destructive personality of the 'servant', and *Accident* (with Dirk Bogarde, Stanley Baker, Michael York, Vivien Merchant and Jacqueline Sassard), the study of a middle-aged man's sexual malaise. Both these films were scripted by Harold Pinter; Evan Jones scripted *The Damned* (1962), an extraordinary venture into science-fiction and the myth of power, *King and Country* and

Modesty Blaise (1966), which satirised the power-and-violence fantasies exploited in the contemporary spy-cult which had invaded British studios more especially in the phenomenally successful Bond series.*

* *Dr No* (1962, Terence Young), *From Russia with Love* (1963, Terence Young), *Goldfinger* (1964, Guy Hamilton), *Thunderball* (1966, Terence Young), *You Only Live Twice* (1967, Lewis Gilbert), all with Sean Connery. Ken Adam's remarkably inventive sets and designs for 'gadgets' and other special effects gradually took precedence in these films. More serious among the spy films have been *The Spy that Came in from the Cold* (1966, Martin Ritt, with Richard Burton), *The Quiller Memorandum* (1966, scripted by Harold Pinter)—both stressing the loneliness of the secret agent left out on a limb—*The Ipcress File* (1965, Sidney J. Furie) and *The Billion Dollar Brain* (1967, Ken Russell), both featuring Michael Caine. The fashion for spy films, sometimes laced with stylised sadism, was preceded by another form of audience self-indulgence in the so-called Horror cult, with extravaganzas in vampirism stemming from the Gothic novels of the late eighteenth century, including the Hammer cycle of films and the more recent films of the former cinematographer, Freddie Francis, such as *The Skull* (1965), *The Psychopath* (1966), and so forth.

Modesty Blaise 1966. Director Joseph Losey
Terence Stamp

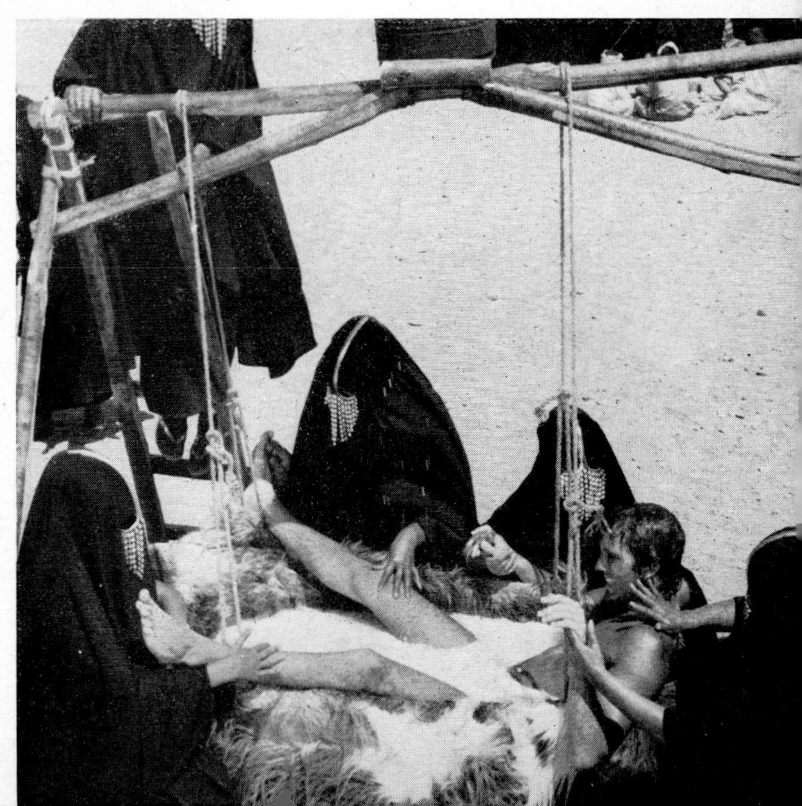

From Russia with Love 1963. Director Terence Young
Daniela Bianchi, Lotte Lenya

Dr No 1962. Director Terence Young
Joseph Wiseman

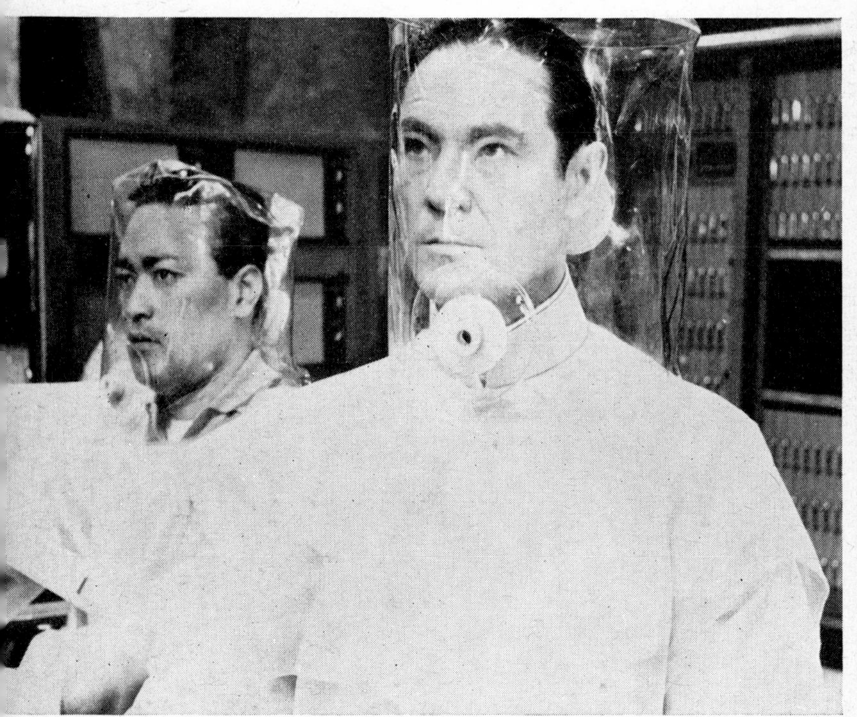

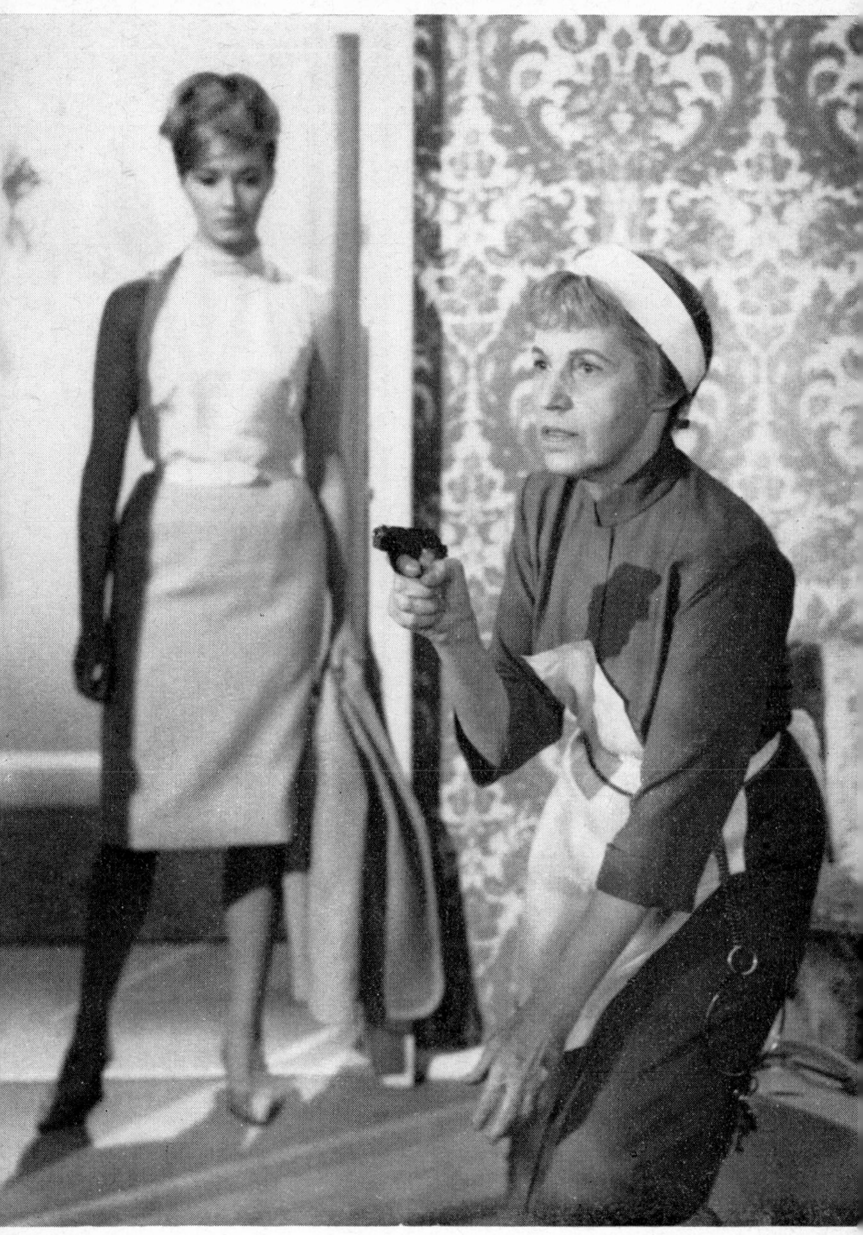

Thunderball 1966. Director Terence Young
Adolfo Celi

Goldfinger 1964. Director Guy Hamilton
Sean Connery, Shirley Eaton

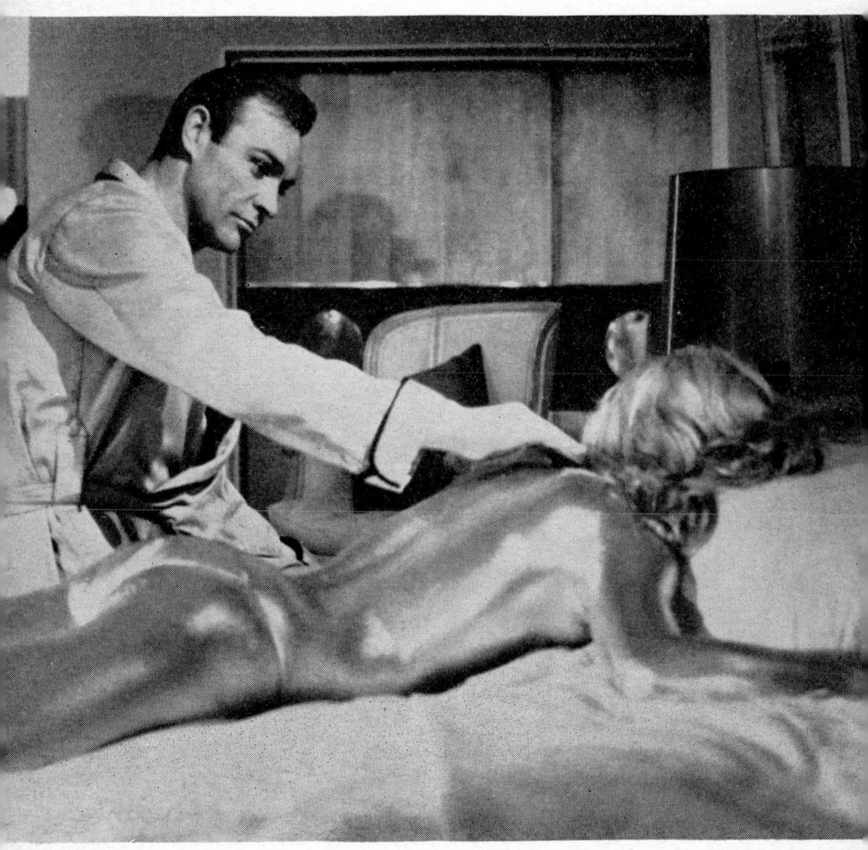

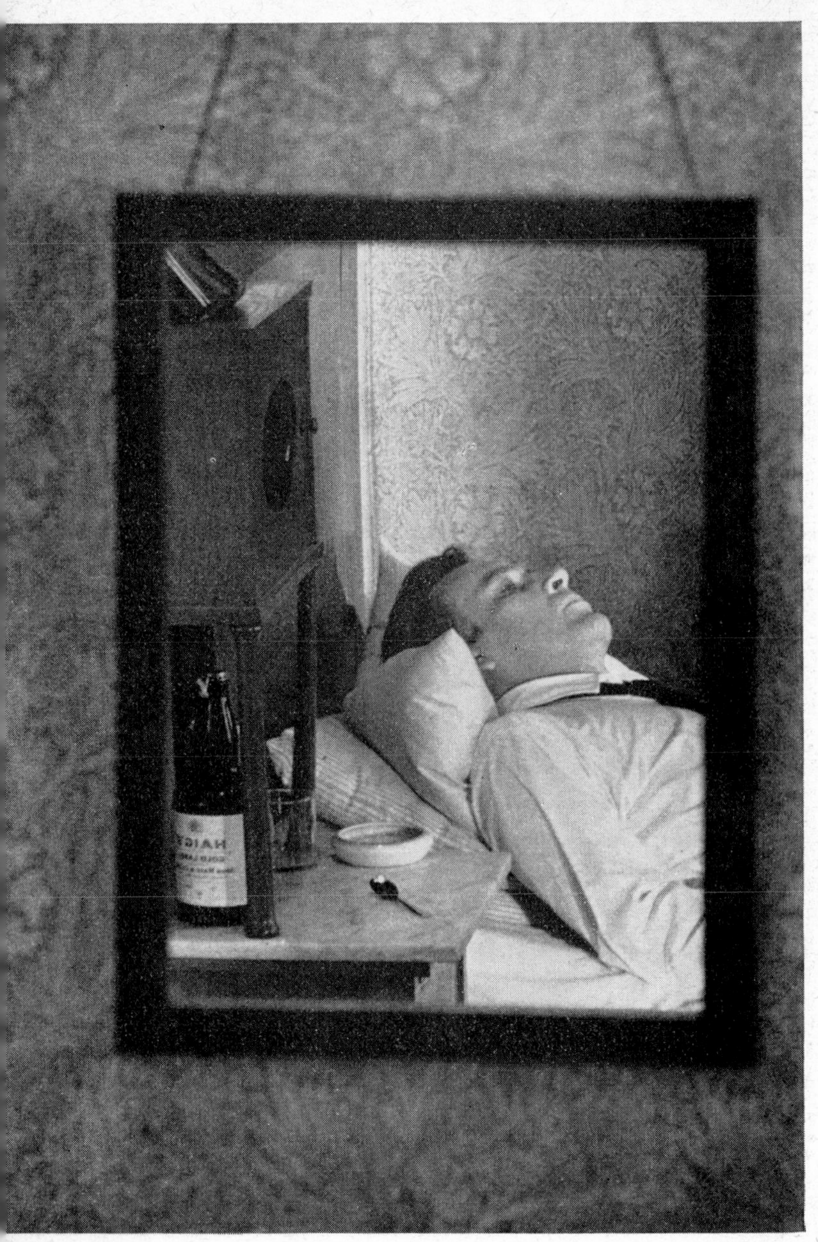

The Spy who came in from the Cold 1966. Director Martin Ritt
Richard Burton

The Billion Dollar Brain 1967. Director Ken Russell
Oscar Homolka

The visitors

Britain has attracted many directors from other countries to come and work, if not consistently over a period of years, like Joseph Losey, at least with some regularity. American directors who have done this include John Huston, Stanley Kubrick, Otto Preminger and Joseph Strick. Huston was among the first to make a series of British quota films—*The African Queen* (1951), *Moulin Rouge* (1953), *Beat the Devil* (1954) and *Moby Dick* (1956). None of these represents the very high level of his best work, but they contain many outstanding performances from stars of the calibre of Humphrey Bogart, Katherine Hepburn and Orson Welles.

Dr Strangelove or: How I learned to Stop Worrying and Love the Bomb 1963. Director Stanley Kubrick
Peter Sellers, Stirling Hayden

The Hill 1965. Director Sidney Lumet

More recently, as we have seen, it has become normal practice for American directors to work in British studios on American-financed British films. During 1967–8, for example, Kubrick, Strick, Sidney Lumet, Fred Zinnemann, and Stanley Donen were among those directing films in Britain. Although there are great economic advantages in this for the visitors, or for their production companies, implicit in the arrangement is recognition of the high technical standards achieved in Britain and, usually, the appearance of British actors and actresses in the films. This has meant British 'nationality' for Kubrick's *Lolita* (1962), *Dr Strangelove, or How I Learned to Stop Worrying and Love the Bomb* (1963) and *2001, a Space Odyssey* (1968), and for Lumet's *The Hill* (1965) and *The Deadly Affair* (1966). It also gave a high

A Man for all Seasons 1966. Director Fred Zinnemann
Paul Scofield

2001 : a Space Odyssey 1968, Director Stanley Kubrick
Keir Dullea

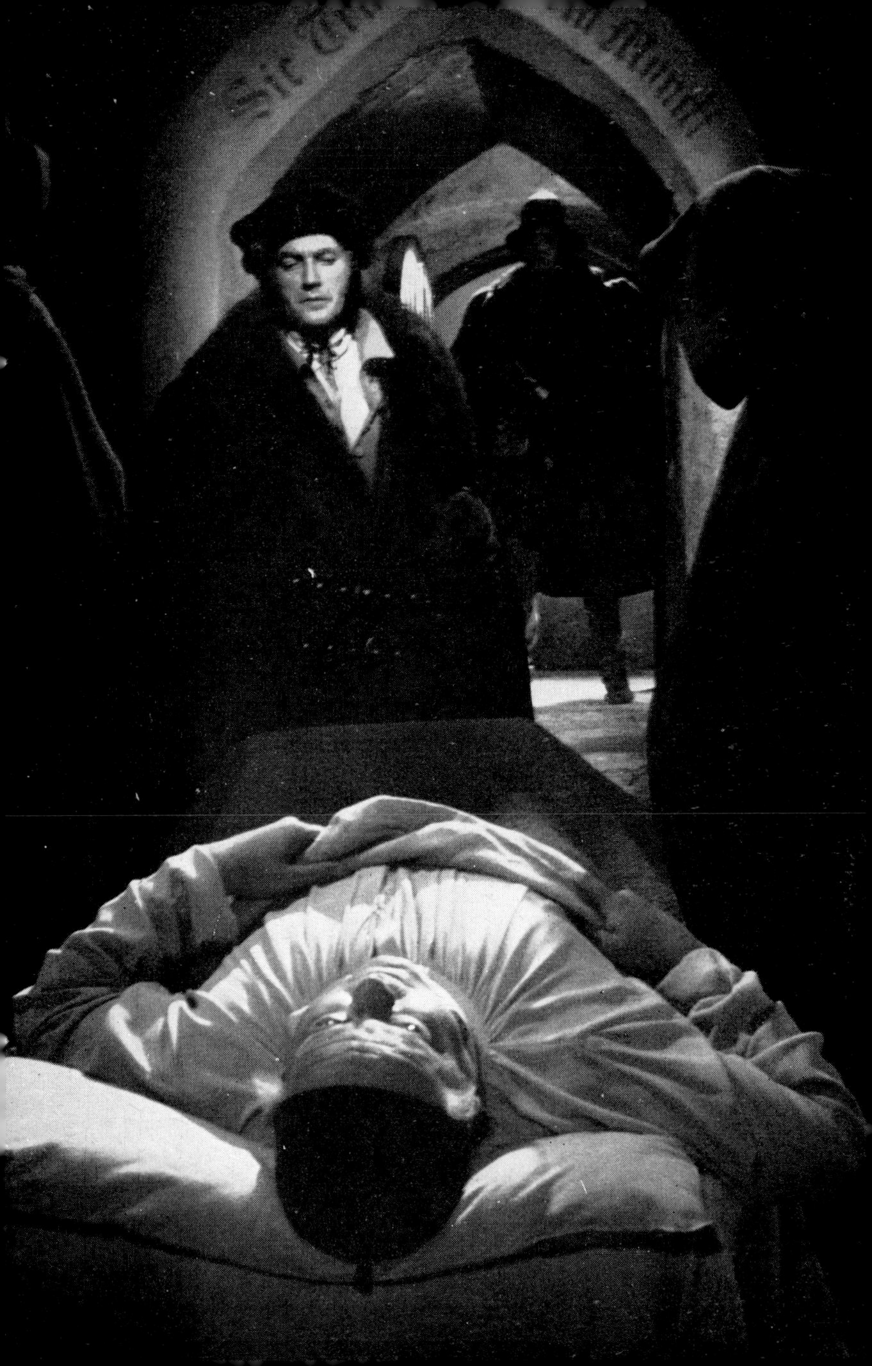

degree of authenticity to Fred Zinnemann's version of Robert Bolt's play, *A Man for all Seasons* (1966, with Paul Scofield and Robert Shaw leading a brilliant cast). This film was designed by John Box and photographed by Ted Moore, who gave a magnificent quality of light and colour to the English landscapes and architecture. The exacting work for Kubrich's *2001*, a unique film technologically as well as in the handling of its subject, was the result of close teamwork between British and American technicians at the MGM studios in Boreham Wood, while the magnificent war-room set for *Dr Stangelove* was the work of Ken Adam.

Joseph Strick's *Ulysses* (1967), shot primarily on location in Ireland, also ranks as a British film. This brave attempt to derive a film from certain veins of action extracted from Joyce's book was for the most part successful as far as it was able to go; the production became over-sensationalised by the censorship issue arising from Molly Bloom's long soliloquy concluding the film, which was unfortunately 'illustrated' by generalised shots which only blunted the effect of Barbara Jefford's fine rendering of it. The film moved from 'actuality' to 'fantasy' like the book, using a continuity of form similar to Fellini's—in which fantasy is superimposed on actuality, an interknit technique which Joyce himself developed in literary terms half a century ago. Strick's achievement, in the circumstances of trying to match the protean scale of Joyce's poetic expression to what he could achieve with camera, microphone, actors and Dublin locations, necessarily reduces this wholly literary scale to what is possible in terms of actual realisation, and the critics differed widely as to the result. But the importance of *Ulysses* lay at least as much in the uncompromising stand taken by Strick over the screening of his film as it did in its quality.

Ulysses 1967. Director Joseph Strick
Milo O'Shea

Among the more remarkable films made in Britain by directors from Continental Europe have been Roman Polanski's *Repulsion* (1965), a startlingly melodramatic exposure of a mentally-disturbed girl's sexual fantasies, starring Catherine Deneuve, the award-winning *Cul-de-Sac* (1966) an uncertainly avant-garde 'dark' comedy in which an occasional brilliance of tragi-comic

Repulsion 1965. Director Roman Polanski
Catherine Deneuve

Cul-de-Sac 1966. Director Roman Polanski
Donald Pleasence

Blow-Up 1967. Director Michelangelo Antonioni
David Hemmings

menace languishes in a story which some critics, including myself, felt to be unsuccessful), and *The Vampire-Killers* (1968), a horror-comic in which Polanski plays the lead in a Transylvanian setting; also François Truffaut's strikingly beautiful version of Ray Bradbury's *Fahrenheit 451* (1966, photographed by Nicholas Roeg), which seemed full of inconsistencies, such as the heroic absurdity (intentional?) of the book-people and the impossibility of maintaining a highly technological society without the sort of 'programming' which would of necessity have to include book-knowledge, or a substitute for it which is neither mentioned nor shown. Poland's most celebrated director, Andrzej Wajda, made

Gates of Paradise in Britain during 1967. Michelangelo Antonioni's *Blow-Up* (1967) achieved an outstanding success; it was the kind of film which proved to be effective on a number of levels at once according to the relative demands of the audience, and its final brilliance lay in its ingenious use of photography itself to reveal the overlap of illusion and the rational in the mind of the modish, self-indulgent 'verité' cameraman, so well played by David Hemmings.

Fahrenheit 451 1966. Director François Truffaut
Julie Christie

Theatre into film

The reliance of British cinema on subjects well-established in other forms is a characteristic already noted. The theatre is naturally enough a source for film 'properties'. Anthony Asquith, for example, specialised in screen adaptations of successful plays which he transferred with a meticulous observation of human behaviour, action and reaction, as the dialogue scenes evolved. His post-war theatrical films, *The Winslow Boy* (1948), *The Browning Version* (1951), *The Importance of Being Earnest* (1952), *Carrington V.C.* (1954) and *The Doctor's Dilemma* (1958) never concealed their theatrical origins, but used the camera to give close and intimate coverage of the original play, expanded a little here and there with a few exterior sequences. Peter Ustinov's beguiling work as a dramatist who is also a producer–director–screenwriter as well as actor led to a warm and pleasingly idiosyncratic entertainment in the adaptation of his play *Romonoff and Juliet* (1961). He was unusually austere in his direction of *Billy Budd* (1962), which he adapted from an American play derived from Herman Melville's novel. It became a moving story of innocence betrayed by the inflexible rules of naval justice of the period, but it was essentially a dialogue-play expanded for the screen. Somewhat like Asquith, Peter Glenville has given sensitive

The Browning Version 1951. Director Anthony Asquith
Michael Redgrave, Brian Smith

The Importance of Being Earnest 1952. Director Anthony Asquith
Michael Redgrave, Joan Greenwood

Billy Budd 1962. Director Peter Ustinov
Peter Ustinov

treatment to the script of Bridget Boland's perceptive play, *The Prisoner* (1954), a study of a cardinal under close communist interrogation, with superb performances by Alec Guinness and Jack Hawkins, and to the later, much more spectacular screen version of Anouilh's play, *Becket* (1964).

More recently, successful stage productions have been moved intact into the studios and filmed with varying degrees of proficiency, but in few cases with any attempt to draw on the full resources of the cinema. Paul Czinner's multi-camera recordings of ballet literally lift the performance from the stage. The most we can claim for Stuart Burge's *Othello* (1967) is that we have a permanent record of Laurence Olivier's unique interpretation in John Dexter's production for the National Theatre. Franco Zeffirelli discarded the normal, theatrical conception of Shakespeare's *Romeo and Juliet* (1968) and put his own strong, restlessly mobile Italianate version on the screen with two inexperienced principals whose youthful good looks and touching

Romeo and Juliet 1968. Director Franco Zeffirelli
Leonard Whiting, Olivia Hussey

The Prisoner 1954. Director Peter Glenville
Alec Guinness

sincerity of behaviour fulfilled the idea of Romeo and Juliet far better than their speech. But whatever is said against it, this Italian production in English with British producers was undoubtedly a film. So was Peter Brook's adaptation of his own stage production of Weiss's play known as the *Marat-Sade* (1967), exploiting a highly-mobile camera and the use of swift and sudden close-shot. *Tell Me Lies* (1968), his expansion through film of *US*, his stage improvisation against the war in Vietnam with bitterly uncompromising lyrics by Keith Mitchell, added group discussion to emphasise the ignorance and lack of informed public reaction to the war as he sees it. Peter Hall in his first feature film, *Work . . . is a Four Letter Word* (1968, an expansion

The 'Marat-Sade' 1967. Director Peter Brook

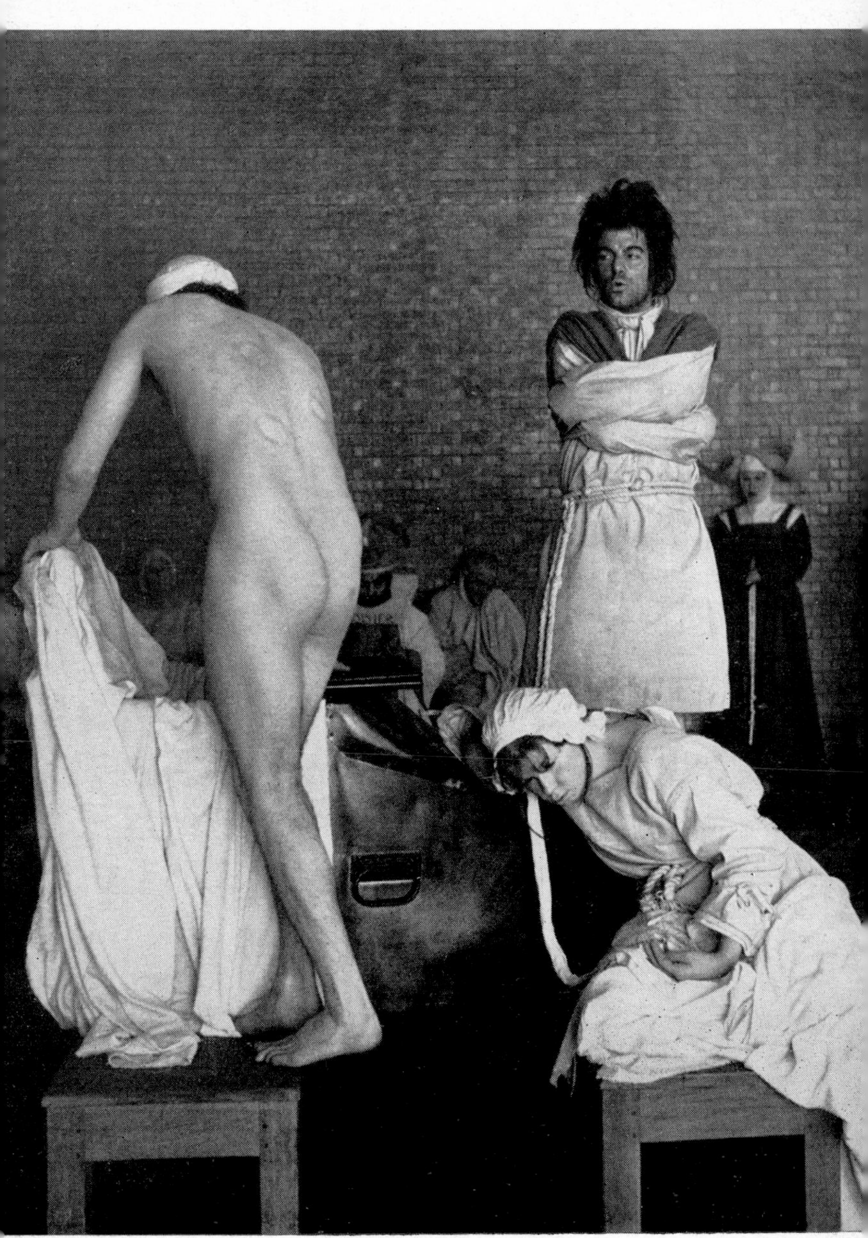

rather than adaptation of Henry Livings' play *Eh*, with David Warner) was a delightful comedy exposing the horror of a fully automated society through the experiences of an unautomatable cultivator of aphrodisiac mushrooms. It only failed when it over-indulged in stock farce. Philip Saville's slow, impressive *Oedipus* (1968) was shot on location in Greece; Sophocles' text, in a modern translation, was spoken with restrained strength, and there was an outstanding performance as Oedipus by Christopher Plummer.

Oedipus 1968. Director Philip Saville
Christopher Plummer

Work . . . is a Four Letter Word 1968. Director Peter Hall
David Warner

Alice in Wonderland BBC Television Film 1966. Director Jonathan Miller
Anne-Marie Mallik

Top gear

Television was to become one of the main sources of new talent for the British cinema of the 1960s; but this time there was an almost complete fusion between the novel, theatre, television and cinema, each providing source-material as well as writing, directing or acting talent for the other. One of the earliest of the senior television directors to direct a feature film was George More O'Ferrall, who had had pre-war experience in the film studios and whose best film was probably the adaptation of Graham Greene's *Heart of the Matter* (1953), with a sympathetic performance by Trevor Howard.

In some respects, it was film-making specifically for television which set a new trend for the cinema, with such outstanding experiments as Jonathan's Miller's *Alice in Wonderland* (1966), and Ken Russell's *Debussy* (1964), *Isadora* (1966) and *Dante*

Gabriel Rossetti (1967). Kenneth Loach's production of certain episodes in Troy Kennedy Martin's and John McGrath's *Diary of a Young Man* (1964) and his productions of Nell Dunn's *Up the Junction* (1965), of Jeremy Sandford's *Cathy Come Home* (1966, the cause of public reaction on a national scale) and of David Mercer's *In Two Minds* (1967) all used film in different ways experimentally to project human experience and personality. Peter Watkins with *Culloden* (1964) and *The War Game* (1965) applied accepted television documentary techniques to imaginary

On pages 136/137
The War Game BBC Television Film 1965. Director Peter Watkins

Debussy BBC Television Film 1964. Director Ken Russell
Oliver Reed

KFB
41

reconstructions of war in the past and the future. It is interesting to recall some of the BBC's brilliant arts' programmes filmed for *Monitor*, with Ken Russell and John Schlesinger among the regular directors. The list of cinema films in production mid-1968 shows that Ken Hughes, Philip Saville, Ted Kotcheff, Christopher Morahan, Elkan Allan, Alvin Rakoff, Waris Hussein, Peter Collinson, Jonathan Miller and Joseph McGrath were all directing features. Similarly, established stars such as Ian Hendry, Michael Caine and Tom Courtenay first became universally known through television, to say nothing of such writers as Harold Pinter and John Mortimer.

Techniques learned from television were soon to be introduced to the cinema. Laurence Olivier did so consciously in the treatment of the soliloquies in *Richard III*. But the television directors themselves brought them in as a natural extension of their work on the bigger screen, as Sidney Lumet, for example, was to do in the American cinema. They appear in Ken Loach's film version of Nell Dunn's novel, *Poor Cow* (1967), with its free-style camera treatment and forms of improvisation which changed the relationship between the audience and the cinema-screen, bringing them closer together (as in television) and inviting them to share in the act of presentation by being witnesses (as it were) when the actress playing Cathy was interviewed about Cathy's experiences and gave whatever answers she personally felt to be 'in character'.

Cathy Come Home BBC Television Film 1966. Director Kenneth Loach
Carol White, Ray Brooks

Released at almost the same time as *Poor Cow, Up the Junction* (director, Peter Collinson) was based on the television play which first established Nell Dunn with the public; Peter Collinson had acquired the film rights himself for only £300.* In *Up the Junction* Polly (Suzy Kendall), bored with her privileged life in Chelsea, deliberately chooses to live and take a job in the working-class environment of London's Battersea; on the other hand, her working-class boy-friend Peter (Dennis Waterman) hates Battersea and tries to live it up by taking Polly for a 'posh' weekend by the sea in what proves to be a stolen sports-car. The tentative love affair collapses through lack of any kind of real understanding and leaves Polly to make what she can of the warmth, the squalor, the frustration and the occasional violence in the environment she has adopted—the presentation of which was the least satisfactory part of this two-hour colour film, which seemed over-blown compared with the spare and ruthless quality of the television original. Peter Collinson's previous film, *The Penthouse*

* One of the principal British films to come direct from a television play was David Mercer's and Karel Reisz's *Morgan, a Suitable Case for Treatment.*

Two unpretentious, but effective films derived from earlier television plays should not be forgotten, *The Small World of Sammy Lee* (1963, scripted and directed by Ken Hughes from his own television play, with Anthony Newley) and *Private Potter* (1963, directed by Casper Wrede, and adapted by Ronald Harwood from his television play, in which Tom Courtenay had originally played). In 1963 James Hill made a brilliant film version of John Mortimer's television play *The Dock Brief.*

Poor Cow 1967. Director Kenneth Loach
Carol White, Terence Stamp

32

The Penthouse 1967. Director Peter Collinson
Suzy Kendall, Norman Rodway, Tony Beckley

(1967, starring Suzy Kendall) was a somewhat distasteful, would-be symbolic portrait of a pair of imposters who violate a girl in the presence of her indifferent lover. More recently he has made *The Long Day's Dying* (1968), a film, part objective, part subjective in technique, which thrusts the violence of the second world war into our faces through the experiences of four isolated commandos, three British and one German.

Another director to start in television (in the USA, Canada and Britain) was Richard Lester; in Britain he directed the famous 'goon' short, *The Running, Jumping and Standing Still Film* and became celebrated as a feature director with his free-style films which appeared in close succession: *A Hard Day's Night* (1964; script Alun Owen) and *Help!* (1965), both featuring the Beatles, and, in between these, *The Knack* (1965, adapted by Charles Wood from Ann Jellicoe's play), which seized the imagination of the festival jury at Cannes and won the Grand Prix. The first film was an engaging romp for the Beatles, half goon-show humour

A Hard Day's Night 1964. Director Richard Lester
Ringo Starr

The Knack 1965. Director Richard Lester
Rita Tushingham, Ray Brooks

Help! 1965. Director Richard Lester
Eleanor Bron

604 ELC

with all the technical trimmings, half affectionate promotion of the Beatles' hallowed image. Its freshness, flung with shameless improvisation into the face of British stolidity, was what endeared it to the critics and public alike. *The Knack*, with gag-variations of the theme of male potency and its limitations, was an unequal film which at its best developed into highly imaginative comic fantasy; it was beautifully photographed by David Watkins. *Help!* became an eclectic raid on every conceivable technical device in the rapidly expanding armoury of the cinema, enriched by the colour possibilities of David Watkins's camera. Richard Lester's next film, *How I Won the War* (1967, scripted by Charles Wood) was officially American; it presents a tragicomic film of the absurd in its handling of the inebriations of war and the starkness of violent death shared like a kind of guilty joke with the audience; the hero, Ernest Goodbody (Michael Crawford), is assigned the dangerous mission of establishing a cricket pitch deep in enemy-held territory in North Africa. One by one the principal characters (including those played by John Lennon, Roy Kinnear and Jack MacGowran) die the inevitable bloody deaths.

Privilege (1967) was the first feature film to be made by Peter Watkins following the success in the cinemas of *The War Game*, which the BBC finally decided against showing on television. It is a courageous attempt to show how organised religion could ally itself with an authoritarian government to win control over a rebellious generation of teenagers. The action is set in Britain during (perhaps) the 1980s, but the trends are those of today carried forward and given a fantastic, ugly twist. The pity is that the film, though wholly serious in its intentions, spills over with in-

How I won the War 1967. Director Richard Lester
John Lennon

congruities which are often confusing and dilute its full impact. The most serious weakness lay possibly in the conception of the character of the pop-singer (played by Paul Jones); it did not seem credible that so debilitated a martyr (a kind of brain-washed Christ-figure undergoing actual torture in public in order to distract his vast, teenage following from the political activities of the authorities) could be led to rebel by the very muted kind of girl-friend Jean Shrimpton was induced to play. However, what mattered in *Privilege* was the skill with which the true satire operated—the fearful PRO (whose statements are similar to the real claims made for Paul Anka in the Canadian documentary, *Lonely Boy*), the teenage girls whirling like weeping dervishes in their ritualised orgasm, the executive meetings at which the pop-singer's 'image' is calculated and planned, the high-level priests

Dutchman 1967. Director Anthony Harvey
Shirley Knight, Al Freeman Jnr

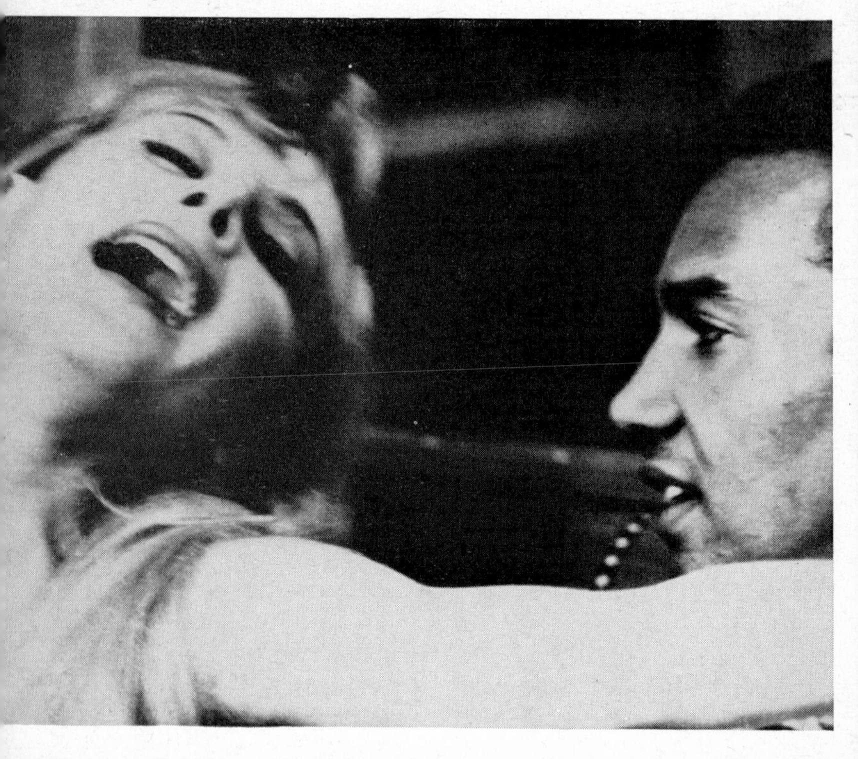

Privilege 1967. Director Peter Watkins
Paul Jones

and pastors adapting themselves uneasily to pop-religion in order to bolster their failing congregations, and the great religious rally itself, which appears a cross between a Nazi congress, a Ku Klux Klan gathering and a session conducted by Billy Graham's preachers and master-singers.

Innovations, however, are by no means confined to the work of directors whose original experience lay in television. *Dutchman* (1967), for example, was an unusual enough subject for a British film. It was the first venture into direction by Anthony Harvey, a highly experienced editor of both documentary and feature film. A one-hour film, its cast of two leading players were both American (Shirley Knight and Al Freeman, Jnr), and it came directly from an American play by LeRoi Jones which sliced into the racial dilemma of white versus black versus white. A sluttish middle-class white girl provokes sexually a quiet-mannered coloured boy

late at night on a train in the New York subway. When he is finally roused, she rounds on him with a tornado of racial invective to which he responds with a pent-up venom going back to the era of the slave-trade. The action becomes a primitive, self-destructive ritual symbolised by the train stopping continually in the same station, and the girl, having shot the Negro, prepares at the end of the film to provoke another. The film, shot in only six days, was a triumphant start to any new director's career; Anthony Harvey allowed it to remain an actor's picture, scrupulously observed by a man who knows how to give both the individual image and the continuity of images their cumulative power. Anthony Harvey then went on to direct Peter O'Toole and Katharine Hepburn in *Lion in Winter.*

In 1964 the incredible story of the production of an outstanding film, *It Happened Here,* came to a partially happy end. It had been begun in 1956 as an amateur film, when its makers, Kevin Brownlow (then a trainee cutter) and Andrew Mollo (an art student and an enthusiatic collector of uniforms and weapons from the second world war) were aged respectively only 18 and 16; it was finished, after only some 40 days of actual shooting and a whole history of exploration into low-budget sponsorship, when both were established professionals aged 26 and 24. The film then made the festivals, but had to wait a further two years before its successful season at the London Pavilion and exhibition in New York, Paris and elsewhere. This remarkable reconstruction of what life might have been like in Britain had Hitler's plan for invasion been successful cost only £7,000 to make, yet for all its success many times its costs were absorbed by distribution and promotion expenses, and the makers netted not one penny; it would certainly never have been completed without financial assistance from Woodfall.* Unfortunately, the distributors insisted on the omission of one, particularly revealing sequence in the film—a genuine improvised discussion between the central character, a nurse who is deluded into joining the British collaborationist organisation, and three people who hold extreme right-wing views, contemporary supporters of these viewpoints, who agreed to appear alongside the actors in the film. These included both professional and non-professional players. The directors also had assistance and advice from former German soldiers and even SS-men.

* See *How It Happened Here,* Kevin Brownlow (Secker and Warburg).

It Happened Here 1964–6. Directors Kevin Brownlow and Andrew Mollo

The White Bus 1966. Director Lindsay Anderson
Patricia Healey

In their varying ways, *It Happened Here* and *Lord of the Flies* did in the end reach their public. At the time of writing, Desmond Davis's study of childhood, *The Uncle*, has not done so in Britain. Scripted by Shelagh Delaney, Lindsay Anderson's *The White Bus*, intended as one section of a three-part film by himself, Tony Richardson and Peter Brook, is a satiric fantasy, with touches of surrealism. It was completed in 1966 but only reached the screen in 1968. The mayor of a northern industrial town proudly escorts a party of tourists round the appalling built-up area of his locality—the monstrous Victorian buildings, the desolate slum clearance areas, contemporary 'developments', everything. The satire is all the more powerful for its overwhelming gentleness, and to ensure visual objectivity, Lindsay Anderson invited a Czech cinematographer, Miroslav Ondricek, to direct the photography. But the problem of the unseen films remains relatively unresolved. It is true that the National Film Theatre, controlled by the British Film Institute, has frequently acted as a shop-window for neglected films; similarly Derek Hill's New Cinema Club, and specialised cinemas run on enlightened 'club' lines, such as the Institute of Contemporary Arts cinema at Nash House and the Paris-Pullman cinema, can act as initial centres of exhibition bringing, perhaps, a small return to the producer in certain cases. But no film, however modestly budgeted, can meet its costs without a far wider range of screening than this represents, even allowing for additional revenue from possible exhibition on television.

These are the problems that have faced the two most enterprising full-length 'off-Wardour Street' productions to be made in Britain in recent years—*Herostratus* (1967, Don Levy) and *Separation* (1967, Jack Bond). Both films use advanced, though differing techniques in presenting studies of psychological breakdown. *Herostratus,* which had almost as painful a story of prolonged production difficulties as *It Happened Here,* was planned as early as 1962 and finally finished (after joint sponsorship by the BFI, the BBC and James Quinn, together with help from many other sources) by 1967. Don Levy, an Australian with a Cambridge doctorate in physics and mathematics, is also a painter who studied film aesthetics under Professor Thorold Dickinson at the Slade; his leading actor, Michael Gothard, was a student at the London School of Film Technique; the photographic team was led by Keith Allams, who achieves spectacularly beautiful results in colour.

Herostratus 1967. Director Don Levy
Michael Gothard

The hero, Max (like the legendary Herostratus who 'demonstrated' by setting fire to the temple of Artemis in Ephesus) seeks the maximum publicity for the public act of suicide he plans in protest against the values of a contemporary society based on destructive self-interest. As a consequence of being caught up in the artificial exploitation of his own campaign by a sadistic public relations executive, he finds his motives changing when it is too late. The subject is therefore in part the self-discovery of a sick man in a sick society. Don Levy, whose previous work in short films had shown a technical virtuosity which sometimes (as in the official documentary about contemporary Britain, *Opus*) betrayed him through sheer flamboyant self-indulgence, produced in *Herostratus* a genuine work of experiment. (And actual experiment is much rarer than the over-generous use of the word would suggest.) He pressed his actors (in particular Michael Gothard and Gabriella Licudi, who plays Clio, the girl with whom Max falls in love) into conditions of prolonged improvised performance carried to the point of a kind of hypnosis designed to reveal subconscious motivation—'extension of the early preparation and recall technique of Stanislavsky,' says Levy. The closeness of the film's visual continuity to the flow of mental imagery was developed technically in order to respond to irrational impulse, and *Herostratus* in consequence is one of the rare films which can truthfully be called surrealist. Don Levy uses long takes, 'threshold', subliminal fast cuts, imagery repeated with variations; the film is made in the form of a cycle, he claims. In spite of its occasional pretentiousness and self-indulgence, *Herostratus* is a most impressive film both technically and psychologically, and in its own way represents a significant expansion of the film as an art peculiarly well adapted to reflect psychological conditions.

Separation (also made on a small budget, but with considerably greater resources than *Herostratus*) was developed out of a story by Jane Arden, who plays the leading part. This is Jane, separated from her husband, Ian, but attended, at least on the level of dream, by a lover. The film is Jane's narrated exploration of her loss and her need. The stated theme of the film is that 'a woman only exists to her full capacity if her image is in some man's heart'. Jane therefore becomes a personification of all women. In her subconscious experience, Jane sees her lost husband as her inquisitor, her perpetual analyst, while her lover, real or imagined, can offer her no depth of affection, only transient and dangerous pleasure.

Separation presents an irrational continuity of action to accompany Jane's spoken search, or research into herself. Once again, the peculiar responses of the film to the imagery of the subconscious are developed by Jane Arden and her director, Jack Bond, with brilliant black-and-white and occasional colour photography by David Muir and Aubrey Dewar.

These exceptional films, it must be hoped, show a new strength where the British cinema has been weakest—in original and imaginative screen authorship. The derivative nature of our films, re-presenting (often with a high creative skill) what has already been presented successfully elsewhere, has been our greatest single limitation. Perhaps the new generation of film-makers, supported by more enlightened policies in film production finance and exhibition, will enable a fully creative British cinema to be born, and discover that there is a sufficient public to make developing production of this kind possible.

Separation 1967. Director Jack Bond
Malou Pantera

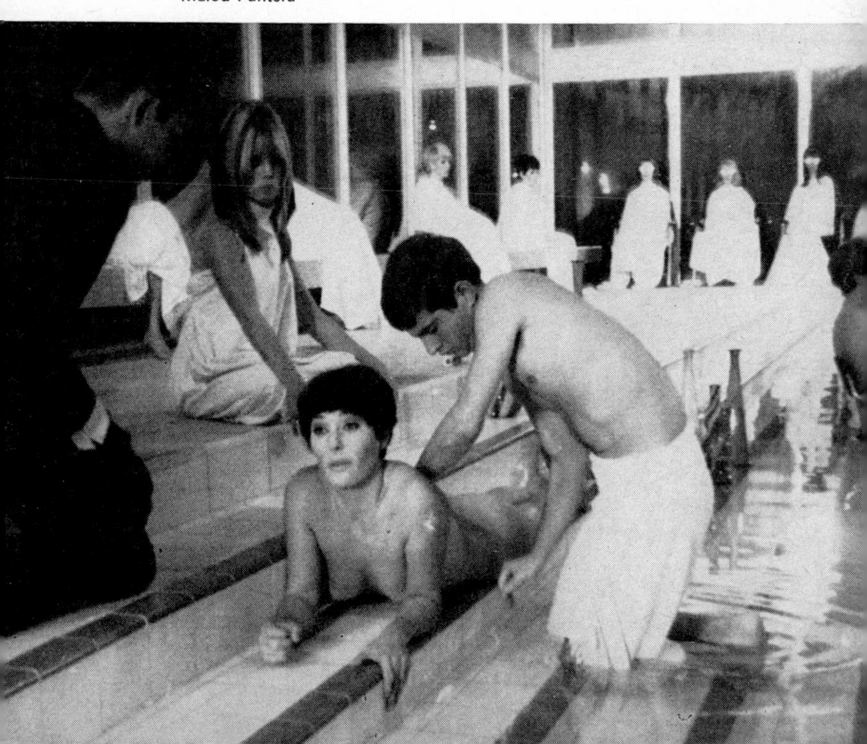

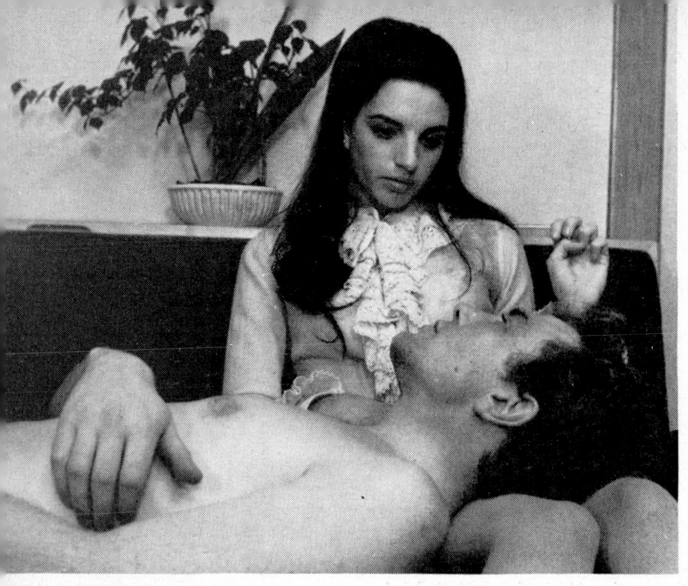

Charlie Bubbles 1968. Director Albert Finney
Albert Finney, Lisa Minnelli

Interlude 1968. Director Kevin Billington
Oscar Werner, Barbara Ferris

Secret Ceremony 1968. Director Joseph Losey
Mia Farrow

Can Hieronymus Merkin ever forget Mercy Humppe and find true Happiness? 1968. Director Anthony Newley
Anthony Newley, Joan Collins

Oliver 1968. Director Carol Reed